Zen Blends

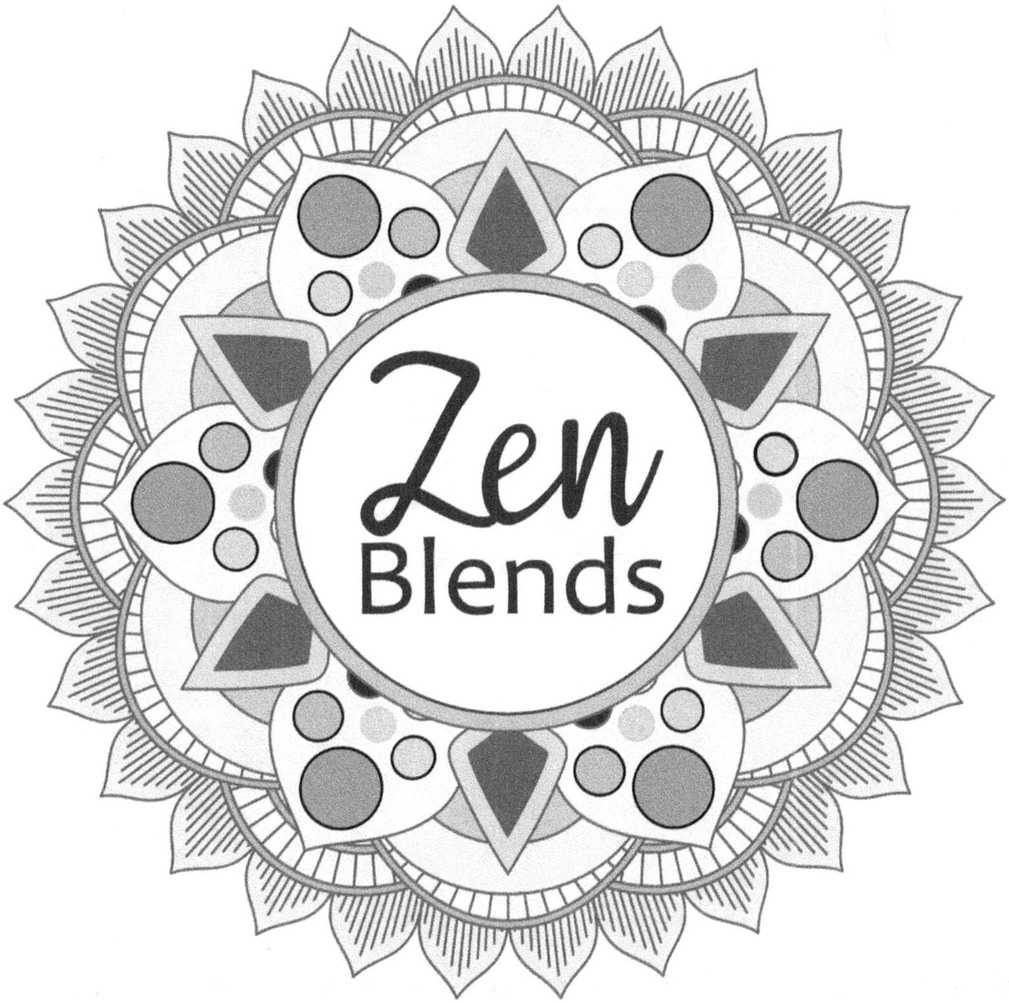

25 Diffuser Blends for Relaxation, Stress, and Meditation
plus 25 more stress relieving coloring pages.

Designed by Catherine Beebe/Escentual Web

© 2019 Dilettante Living Publications
ISBN: 978-1-951554-03-3

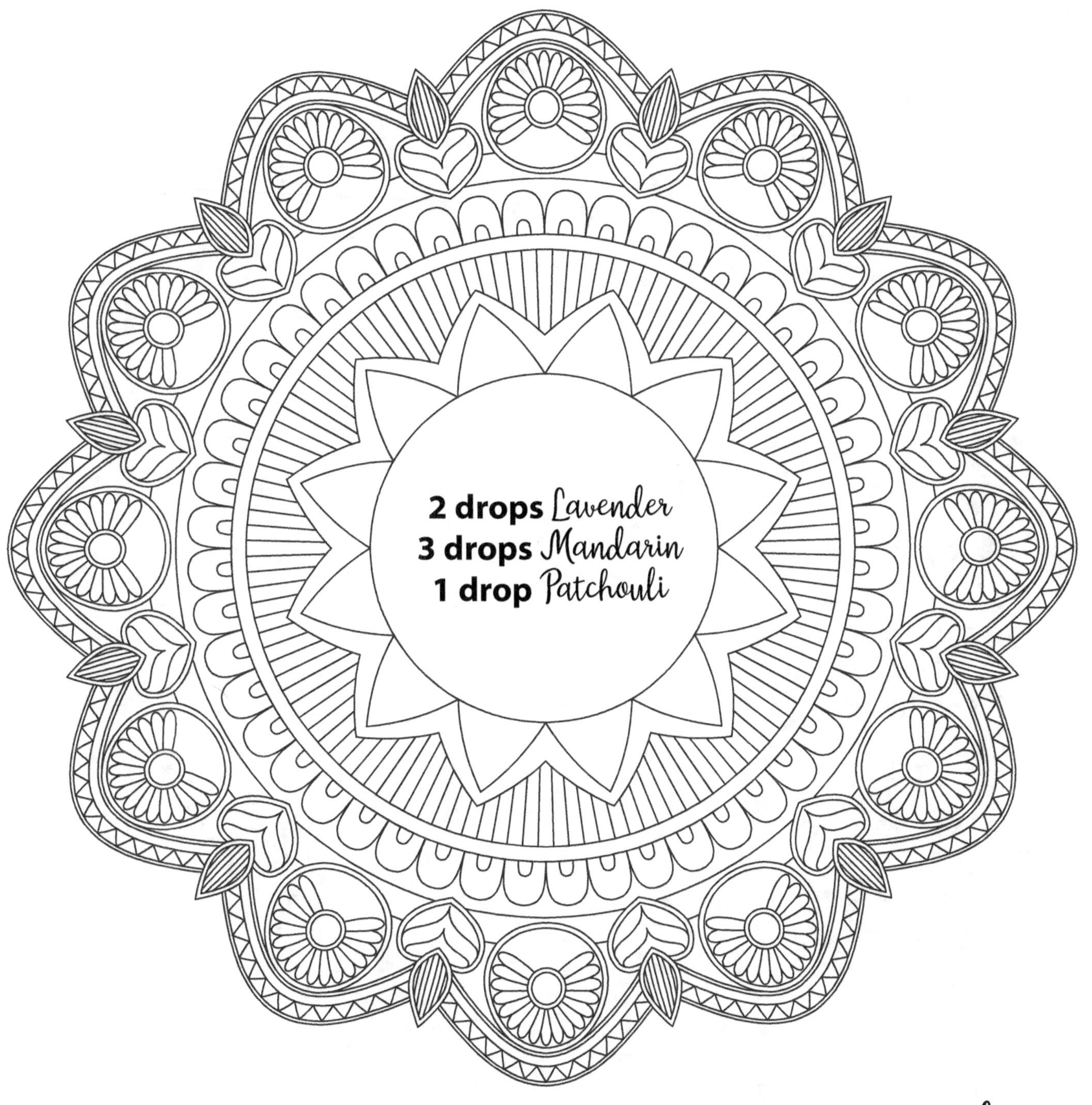

Calming

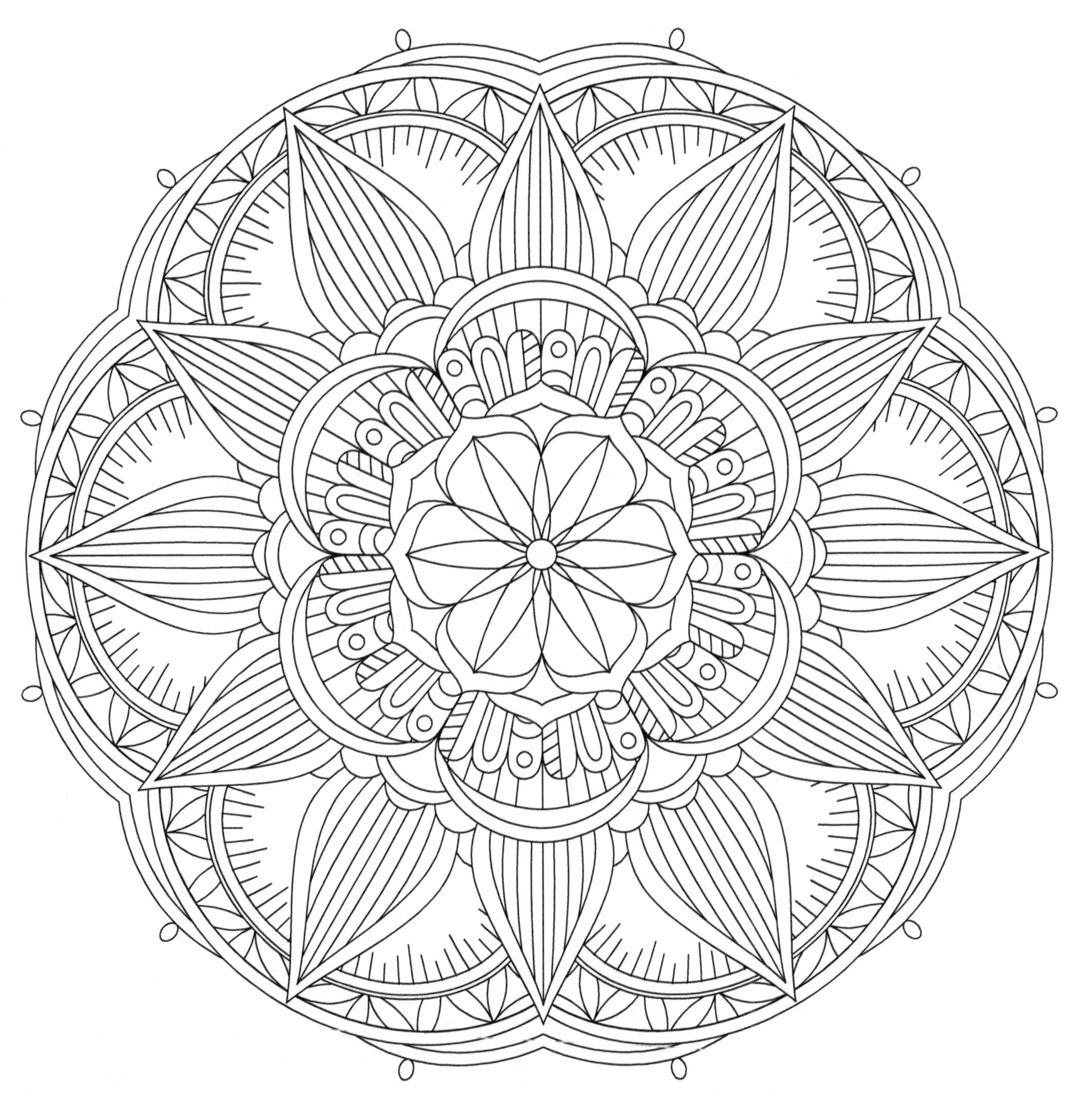

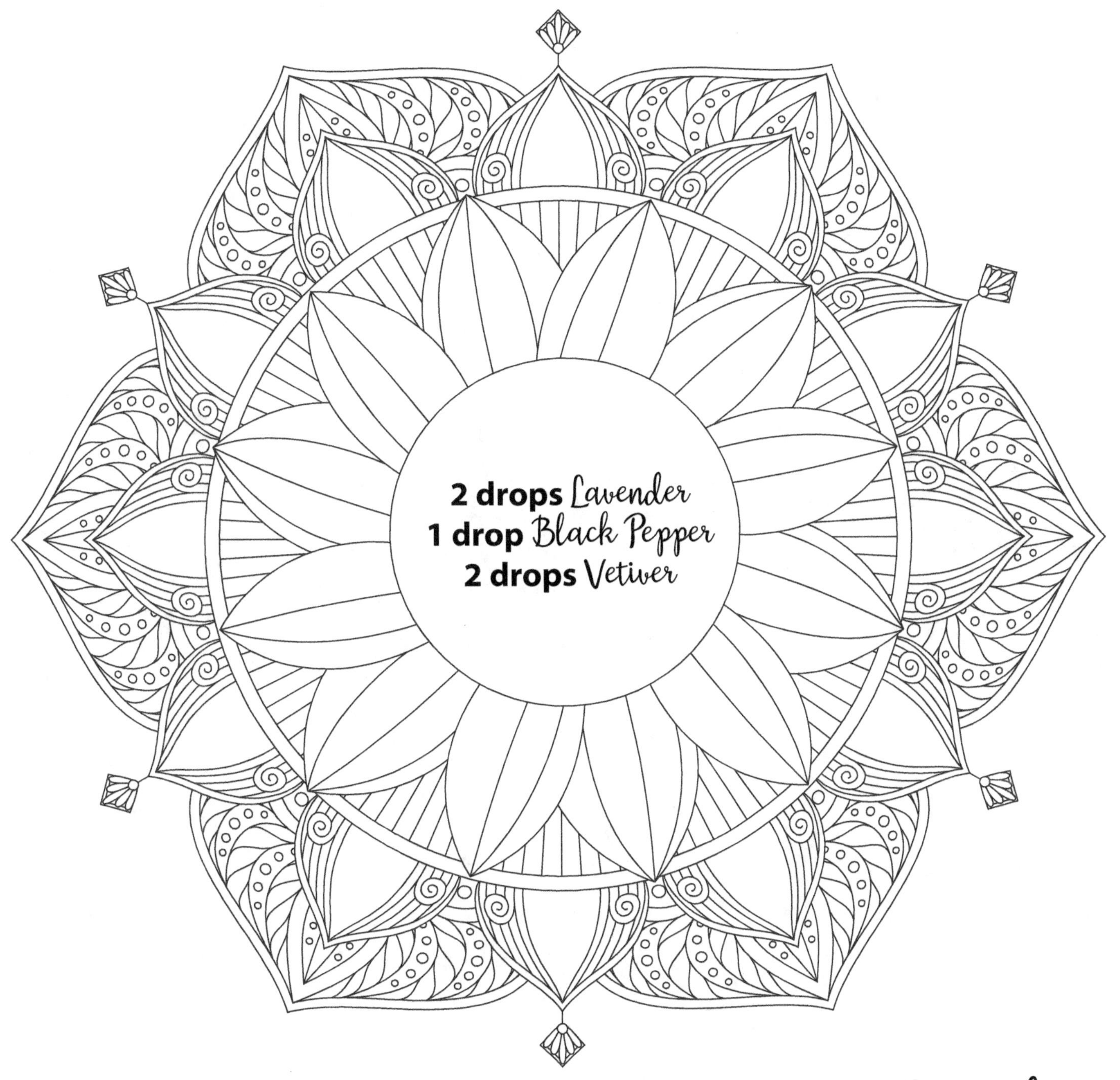

Grounding

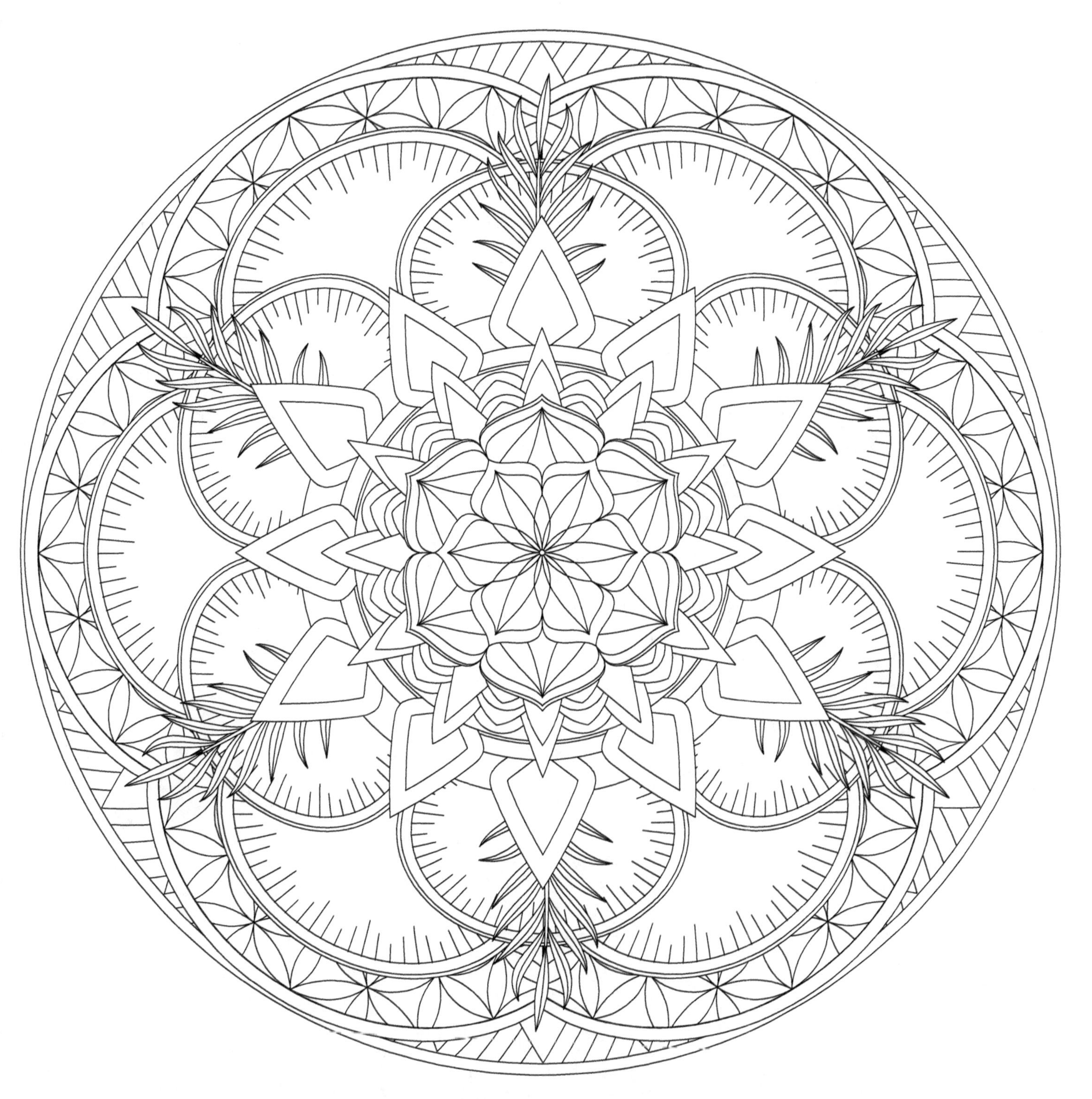

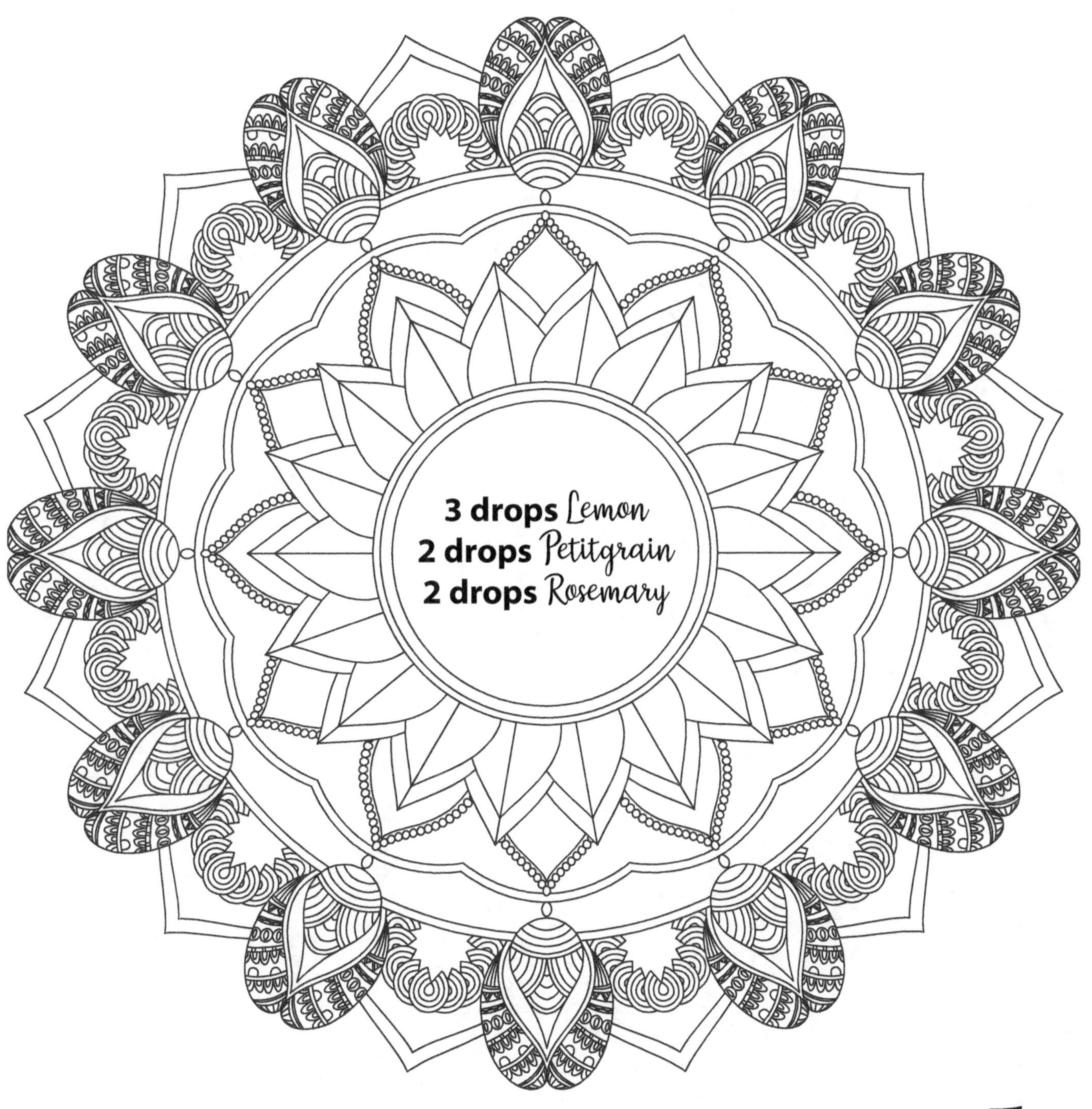

Focus

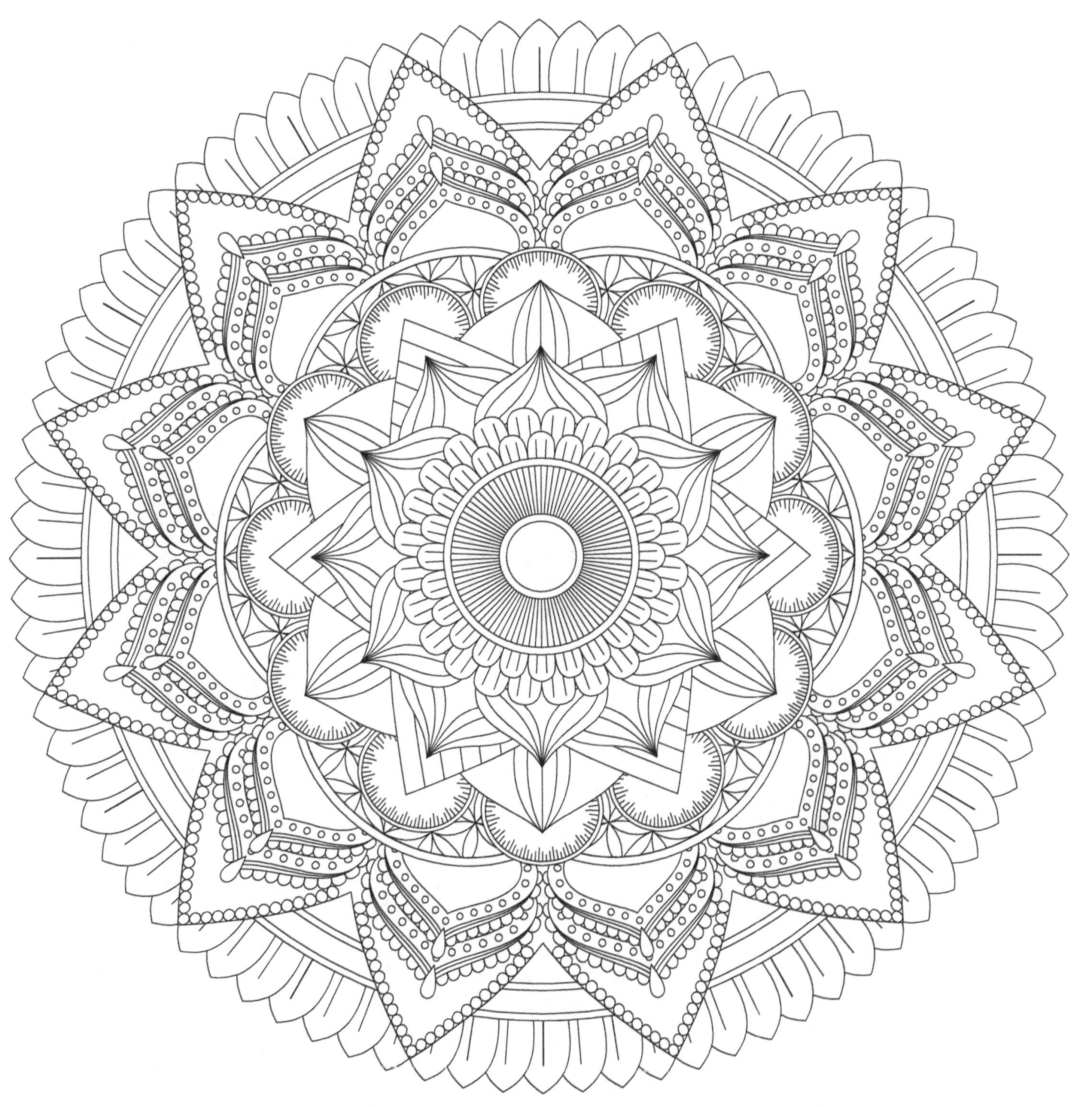

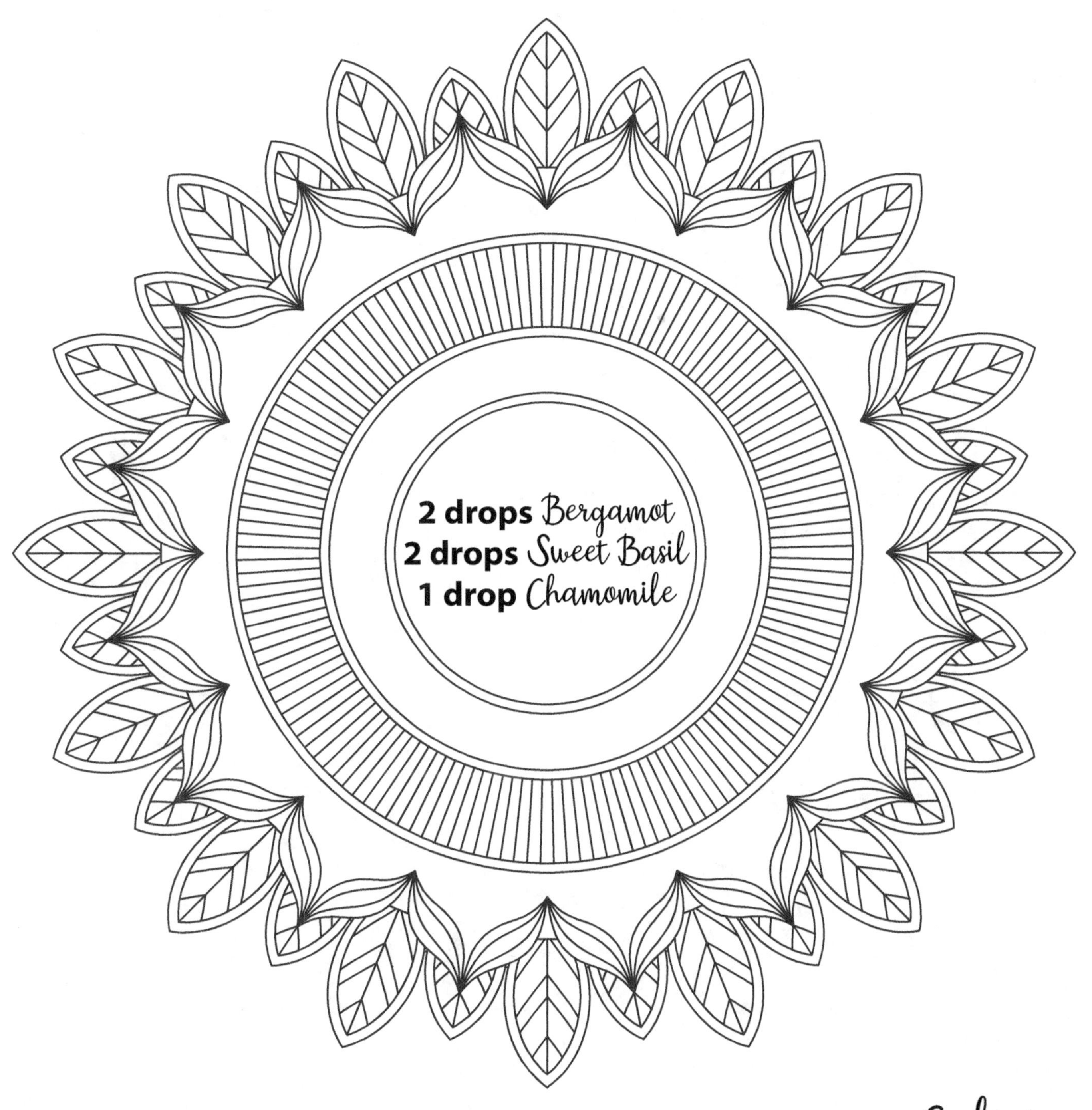

Calming

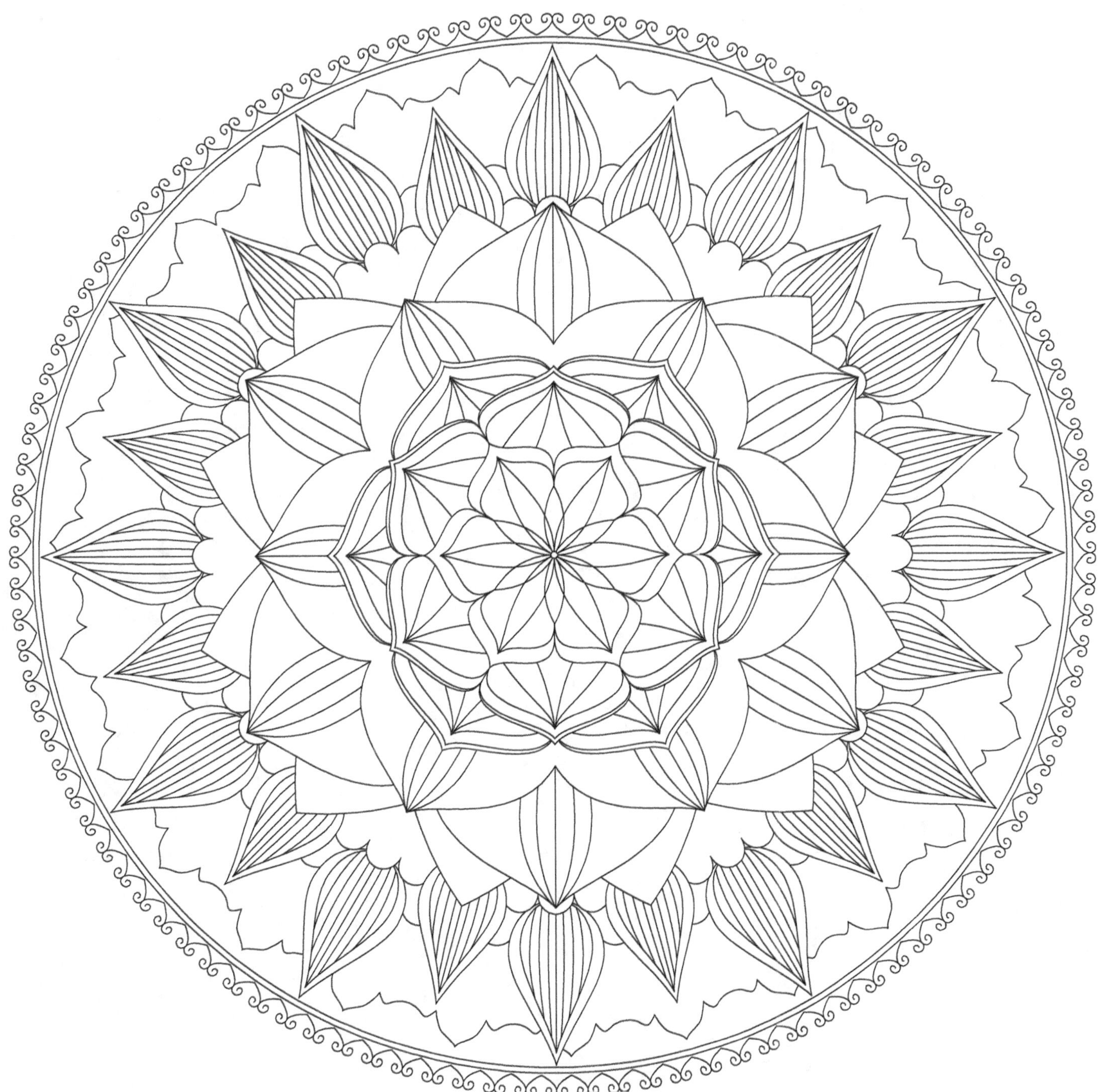

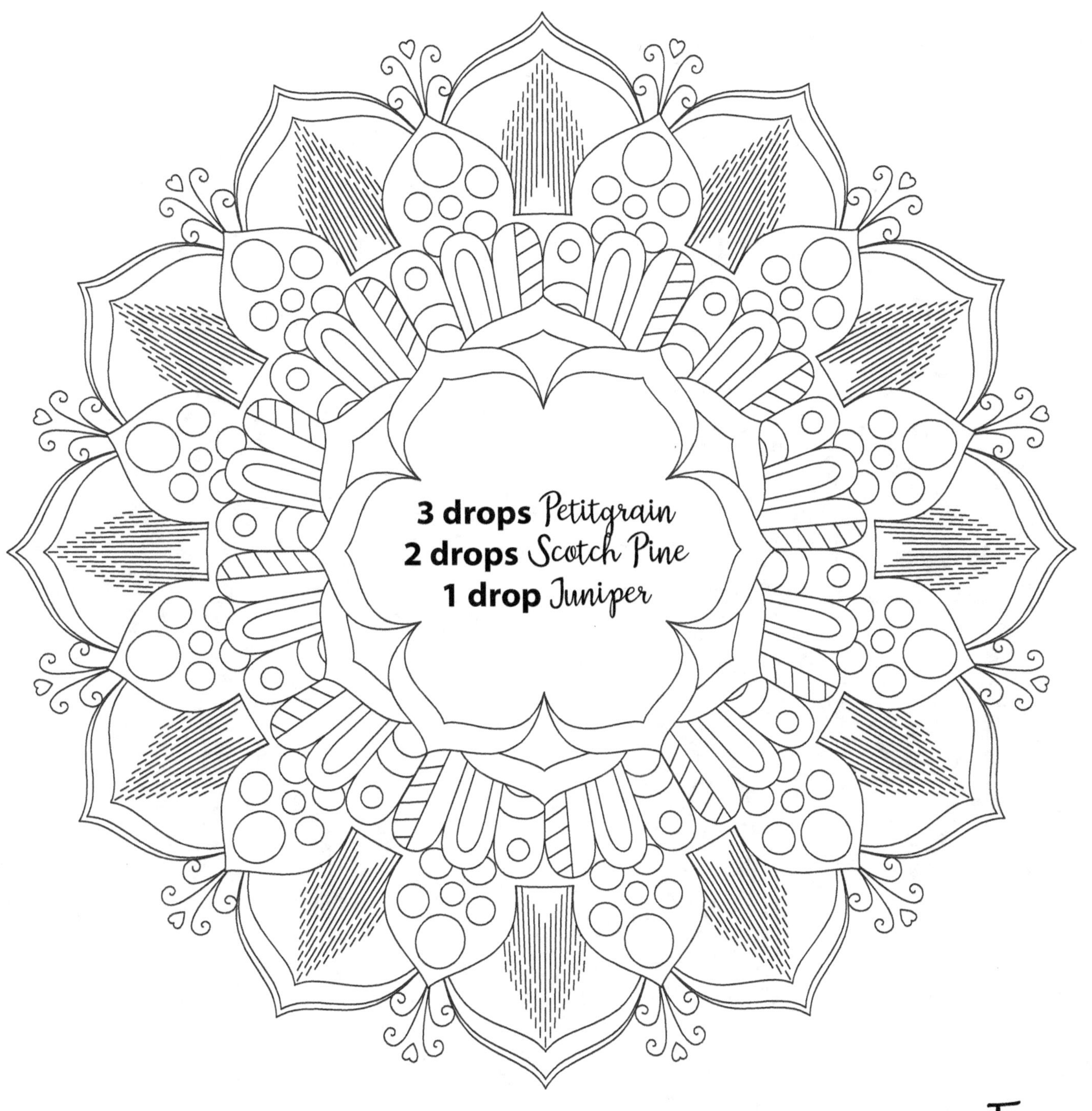

Focus

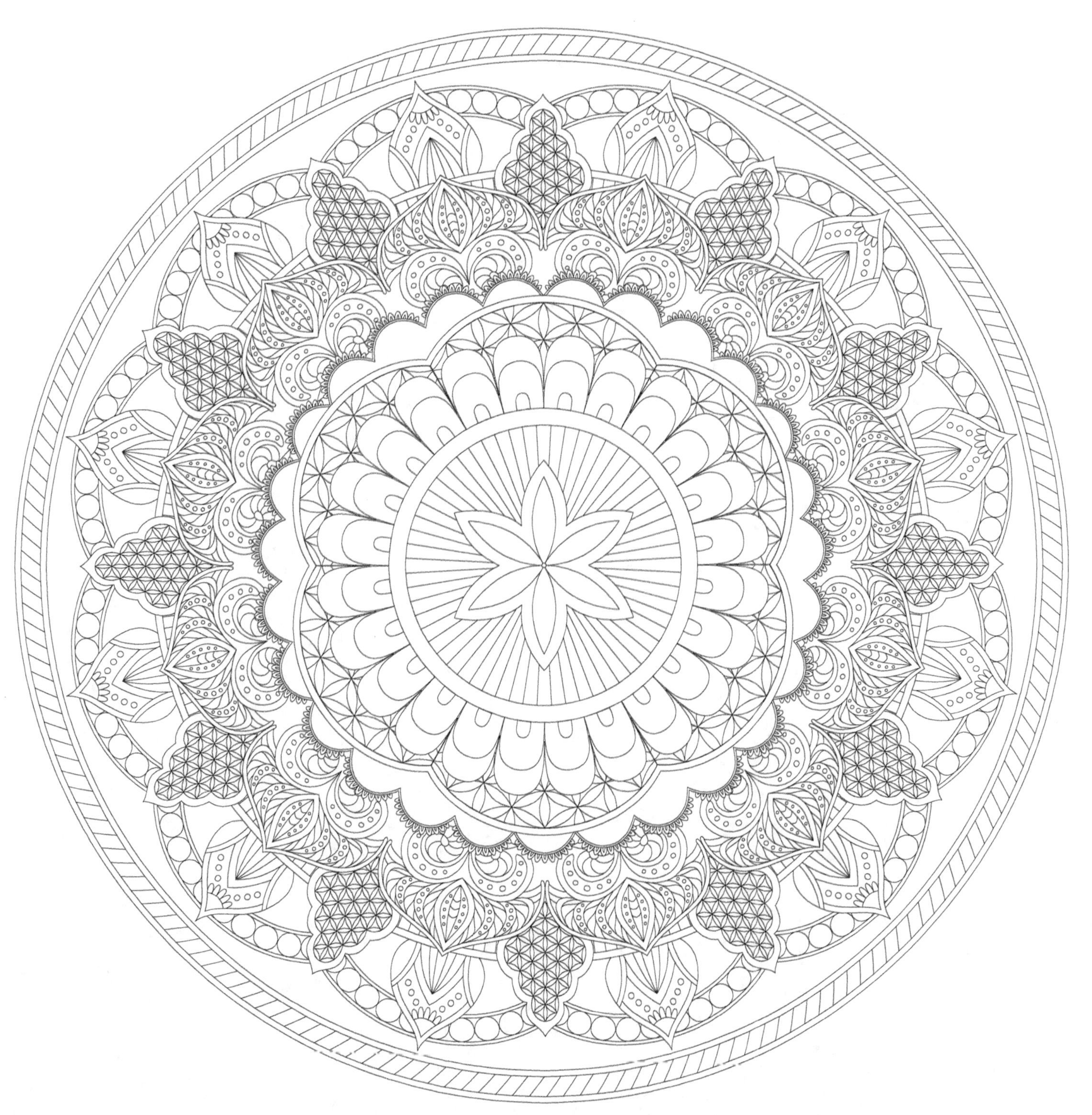

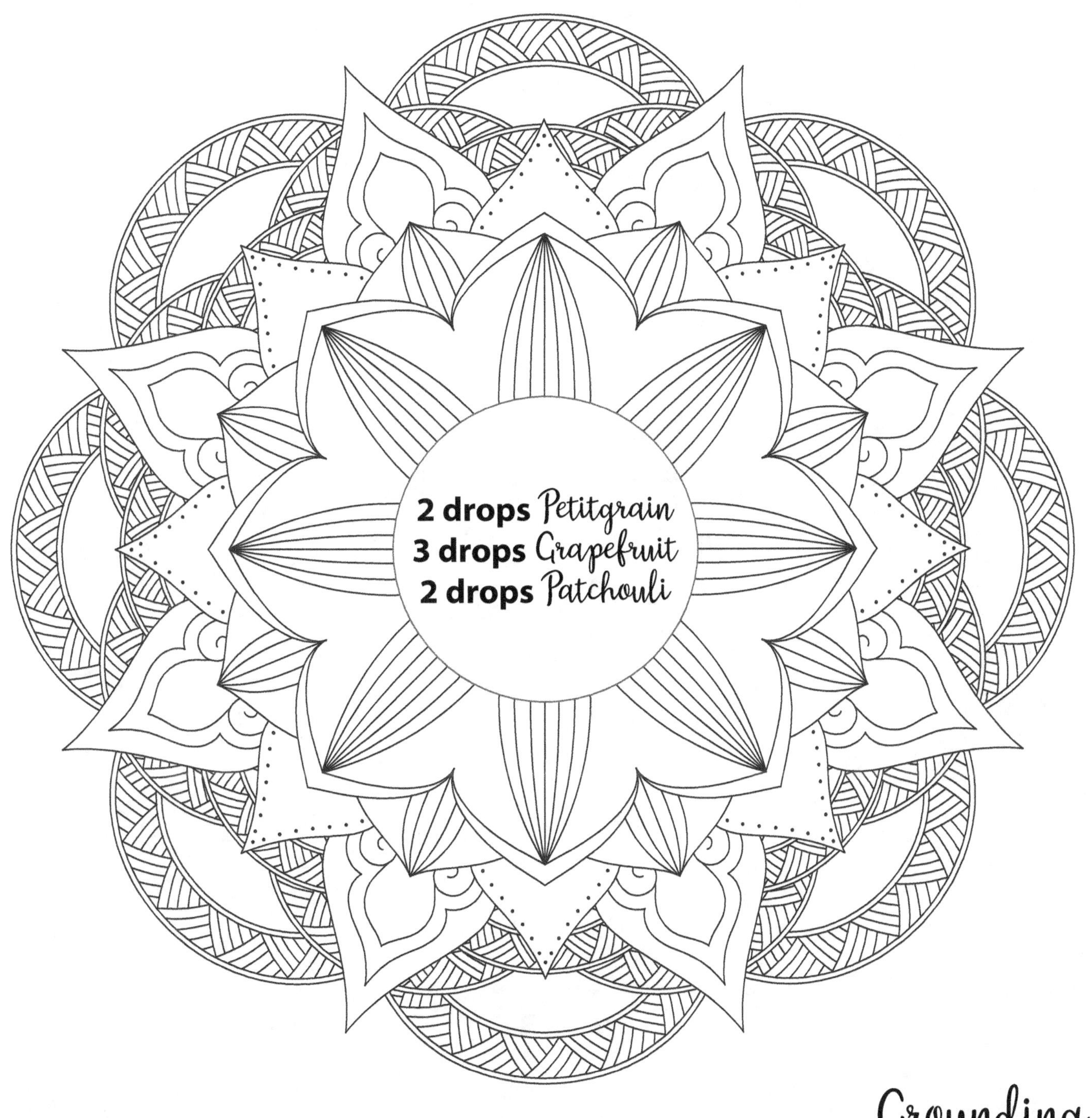

2 drops Petitgrain
3 drops Grapefruit
2 drops Patchouli
Grounding

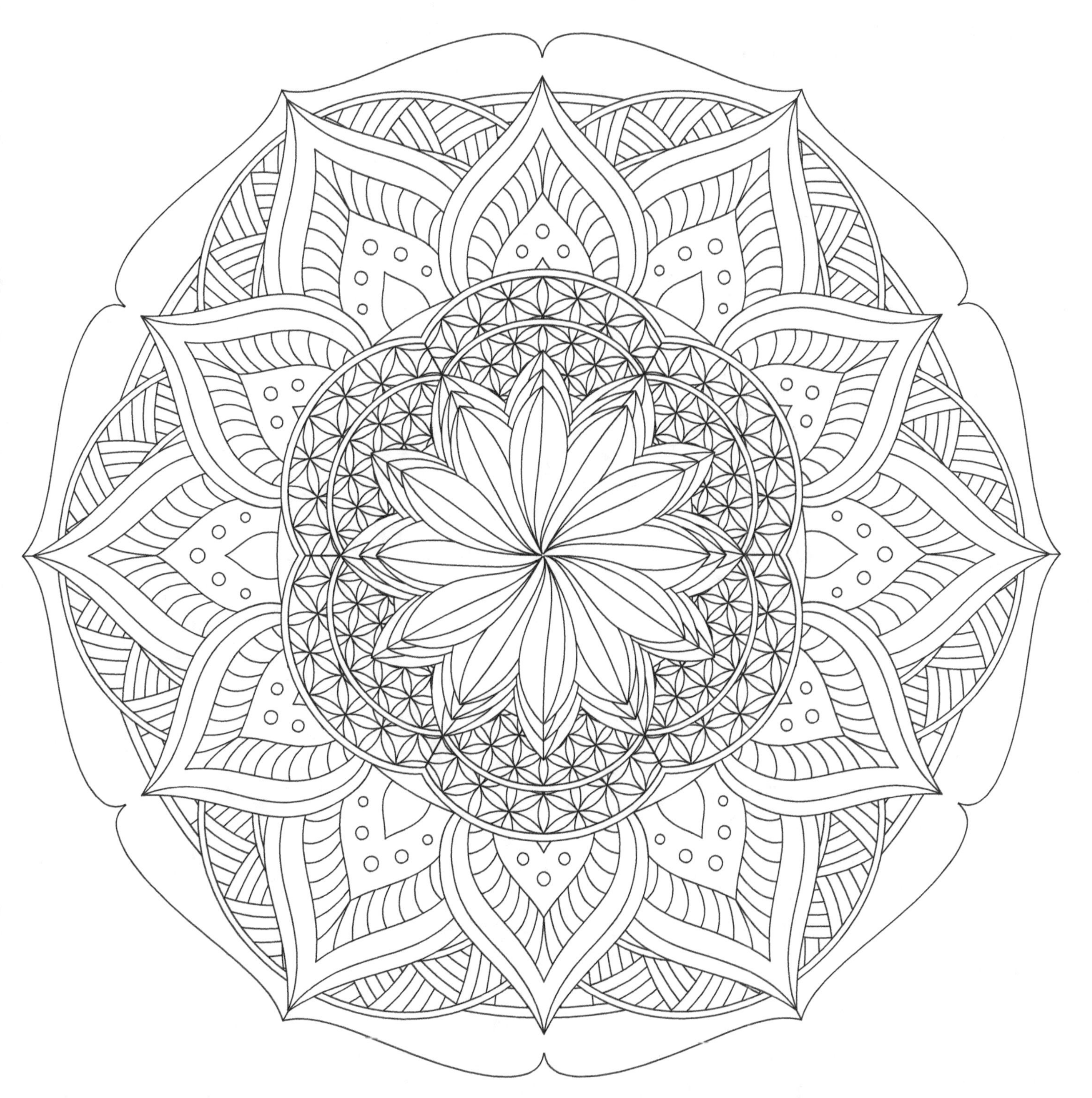

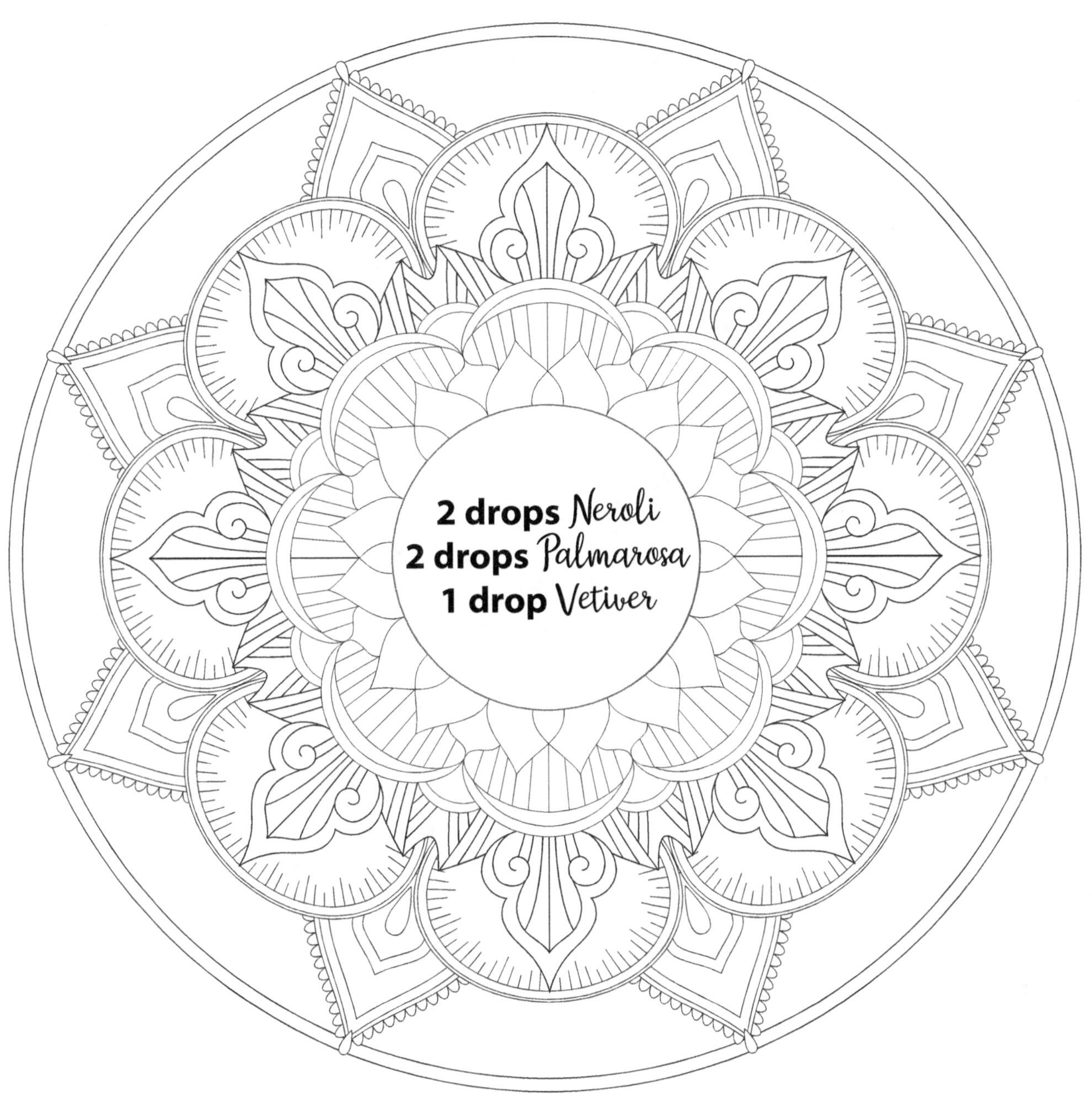

De-Stress

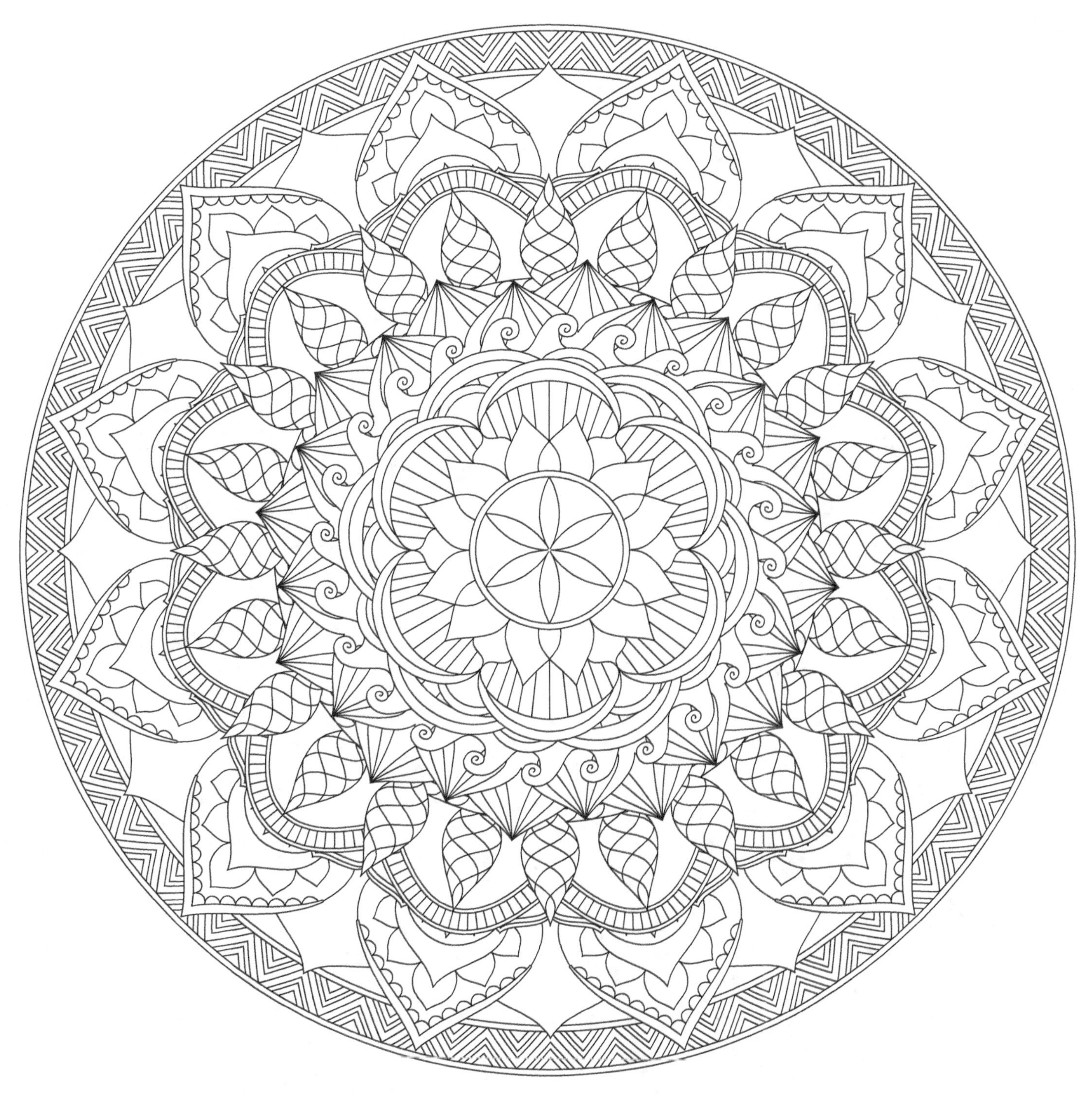

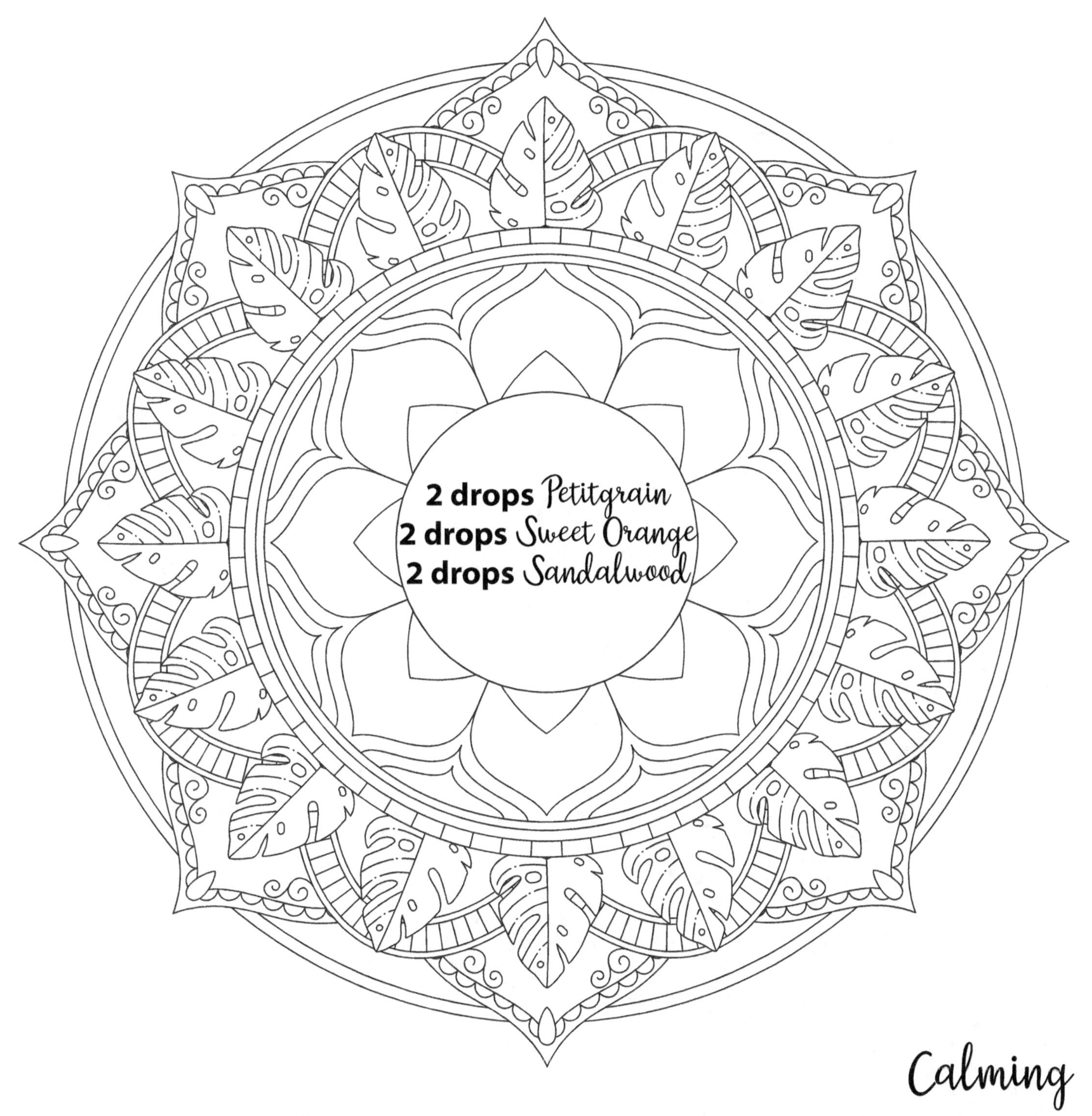

2 drops Petitgrain
2 drops Sweet Orange
2 drops Sandalwood
Calming

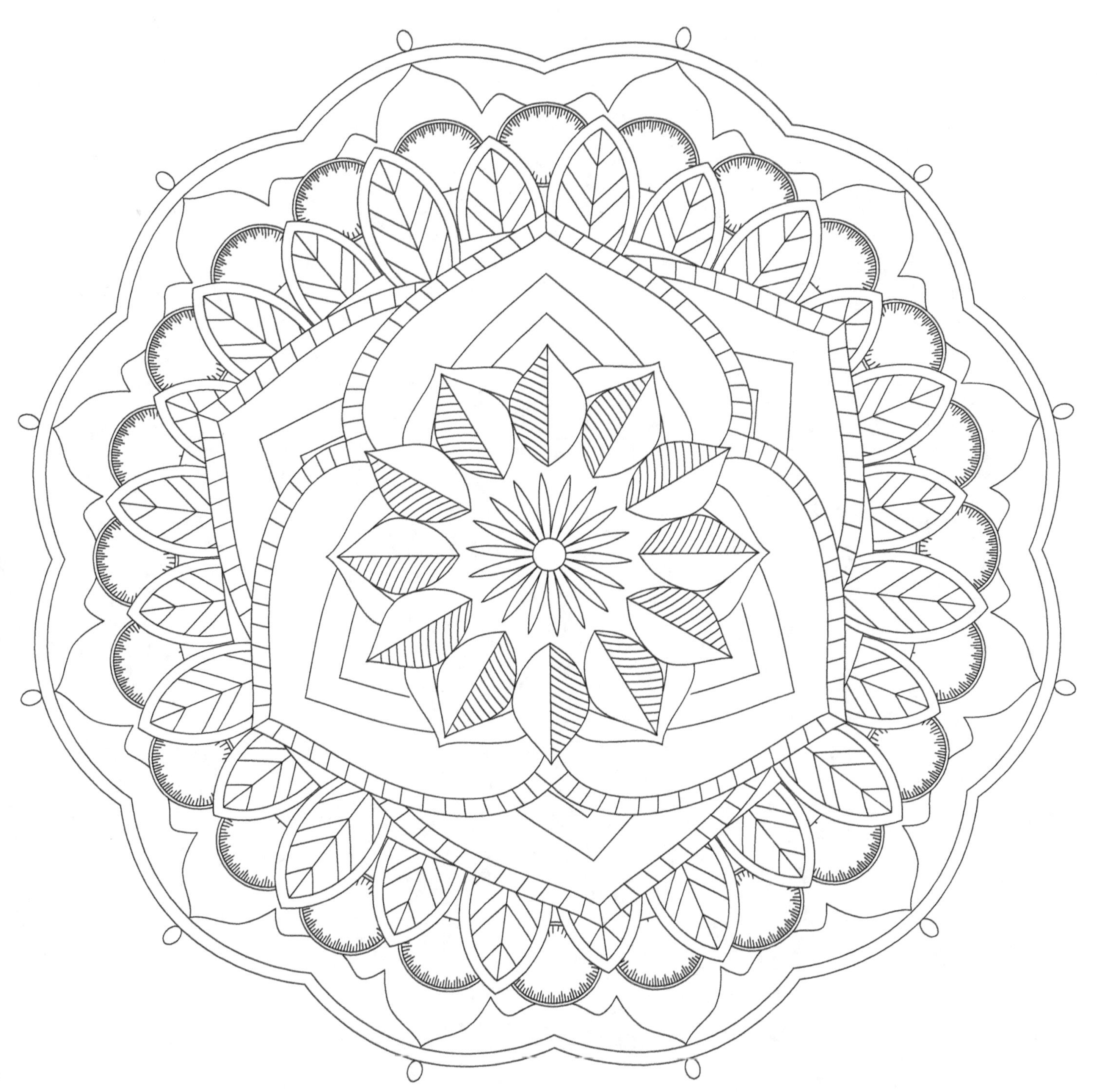

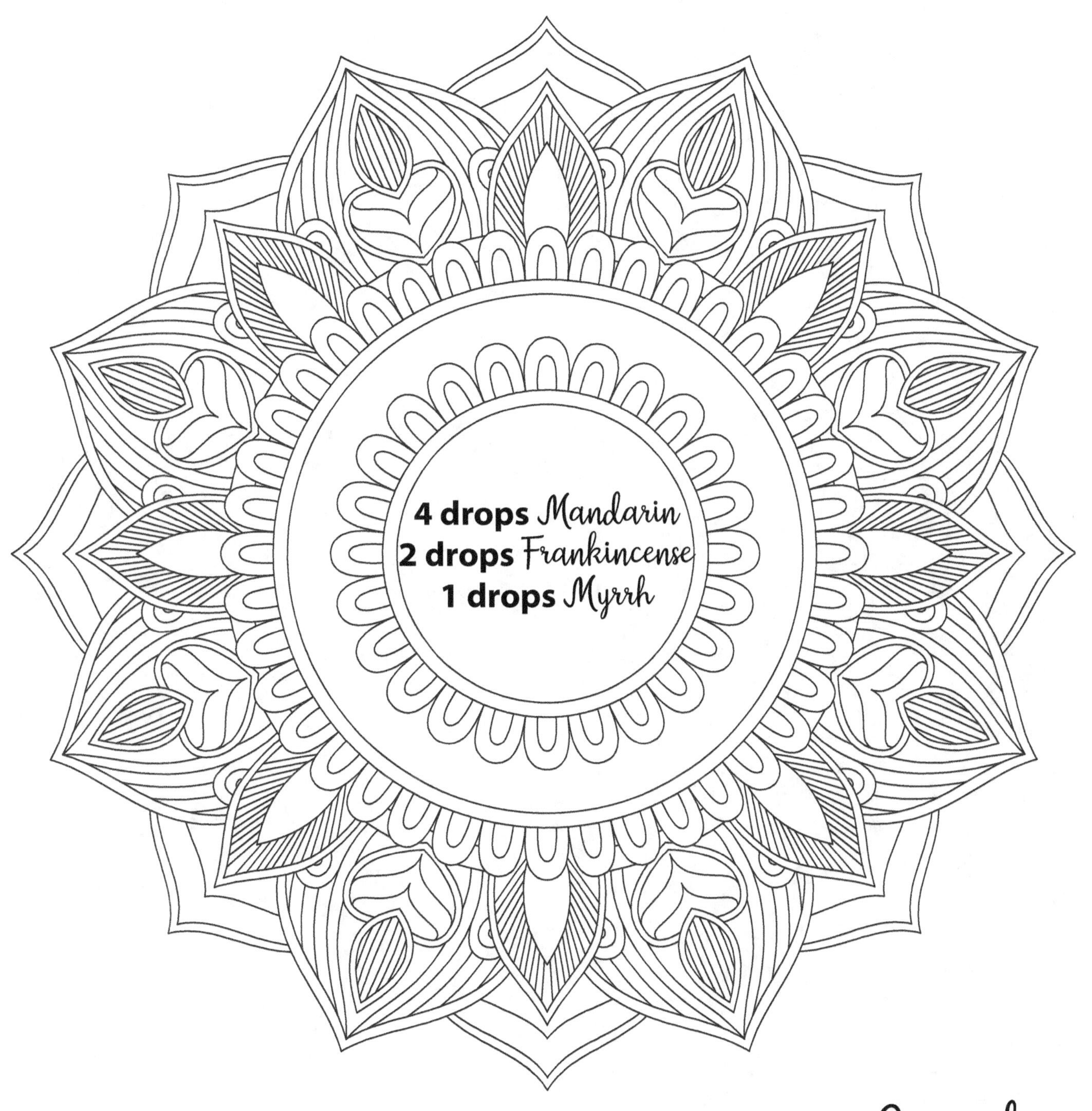
4 drops Mandarin
2 drops Frankincense
1 drops Myrrh
Grounding

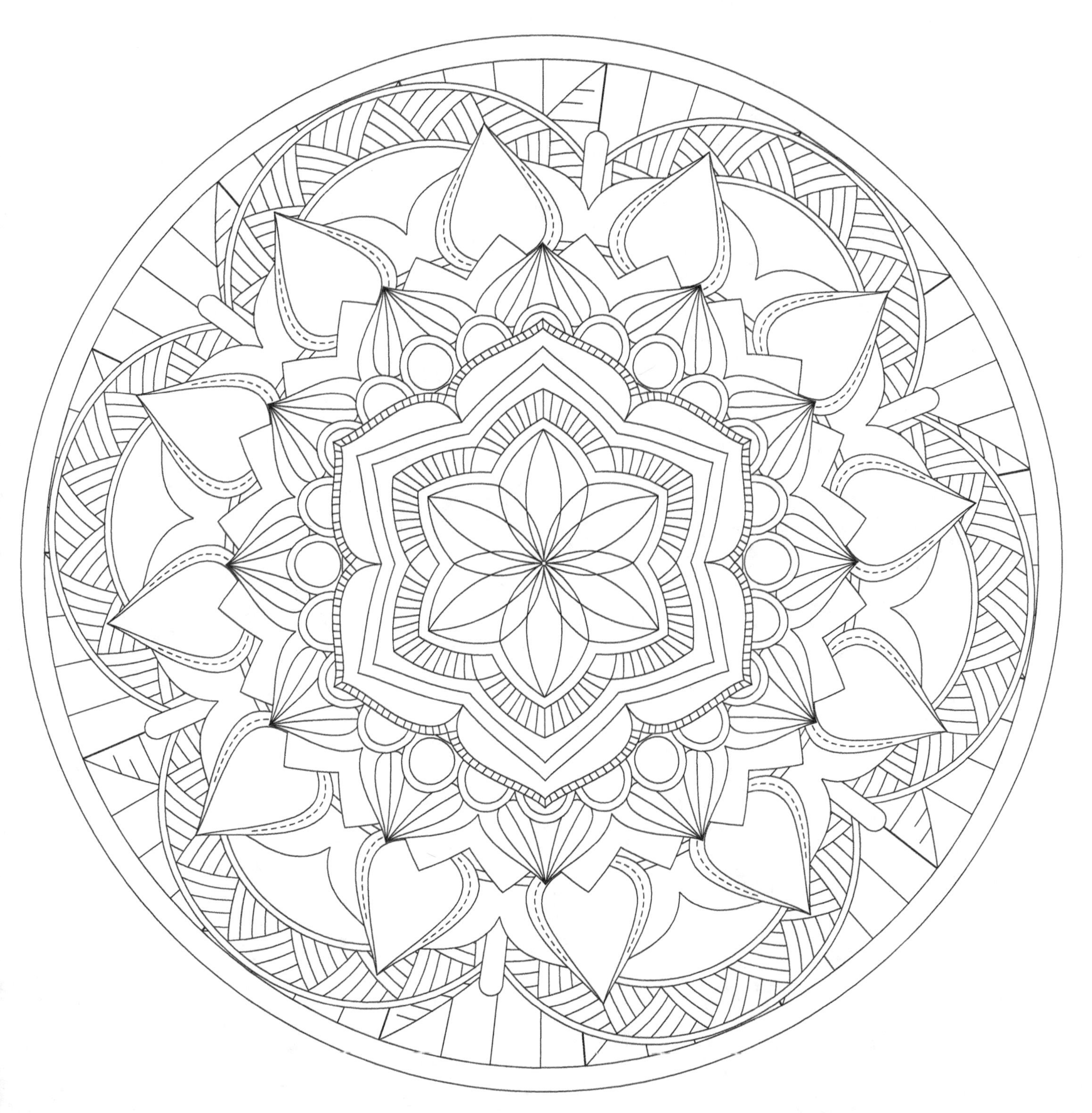

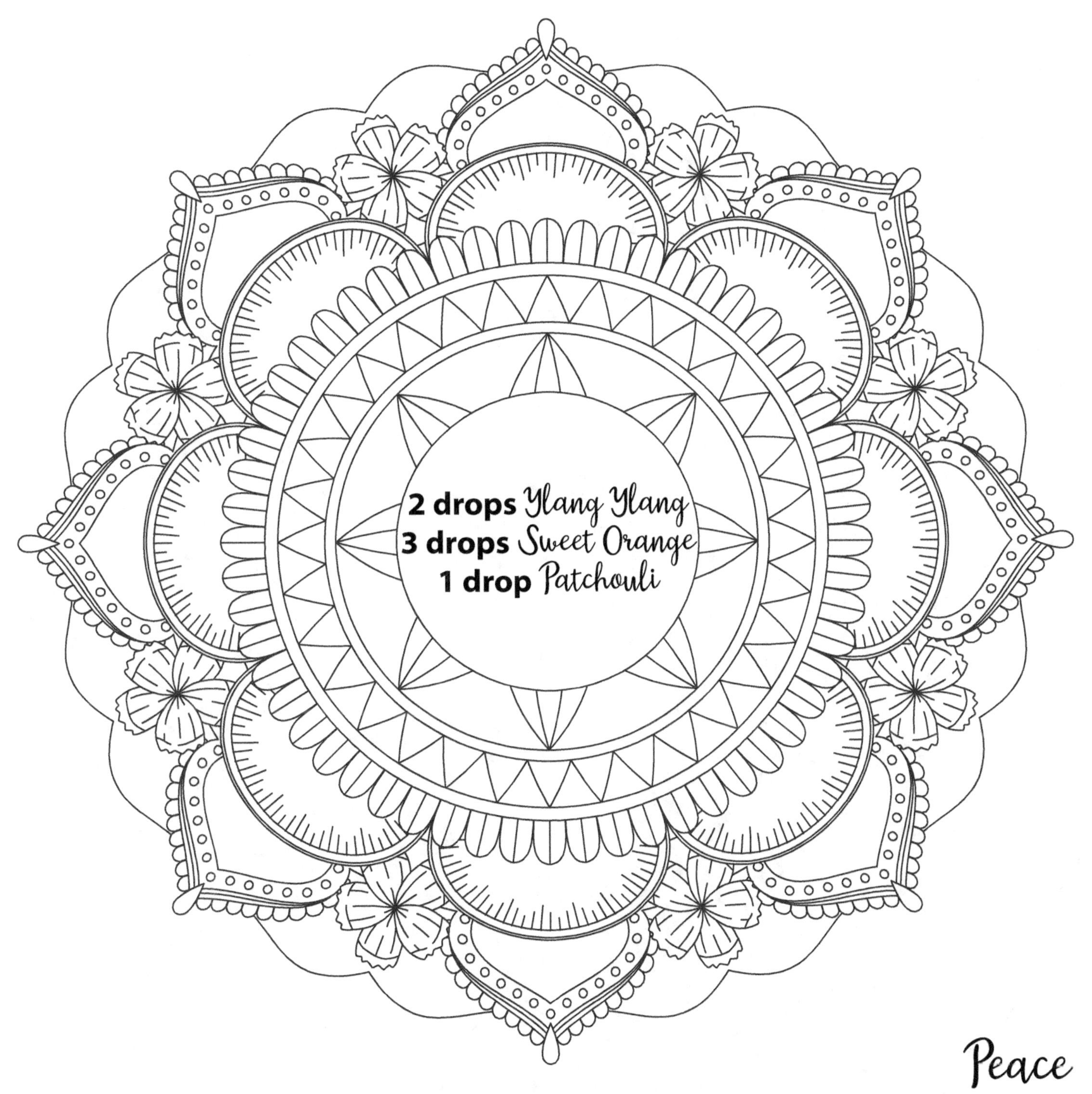

2 drops Ylang Ylang
3 drops Sweet Orange
1 drop Patchouli
Peace

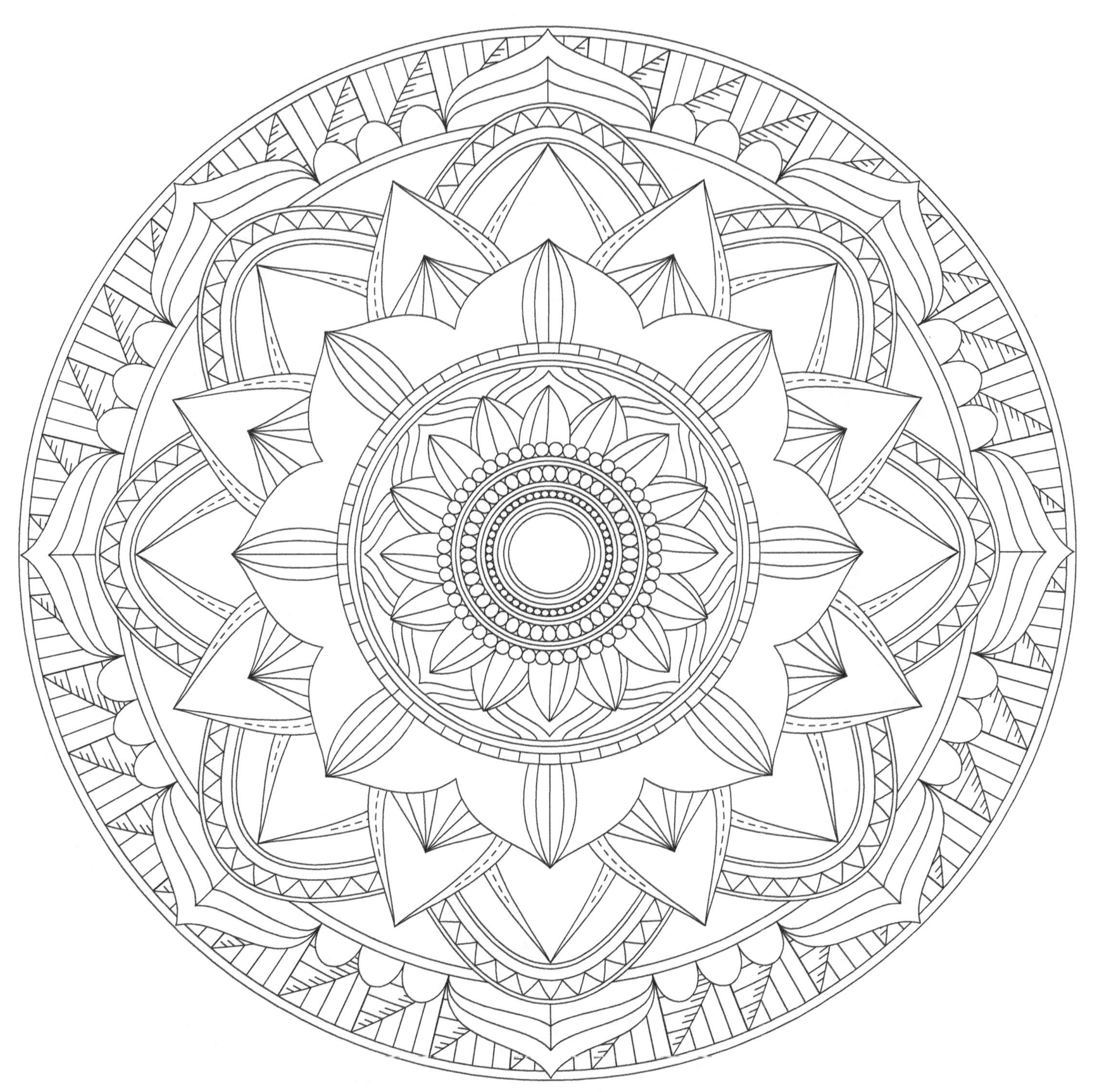

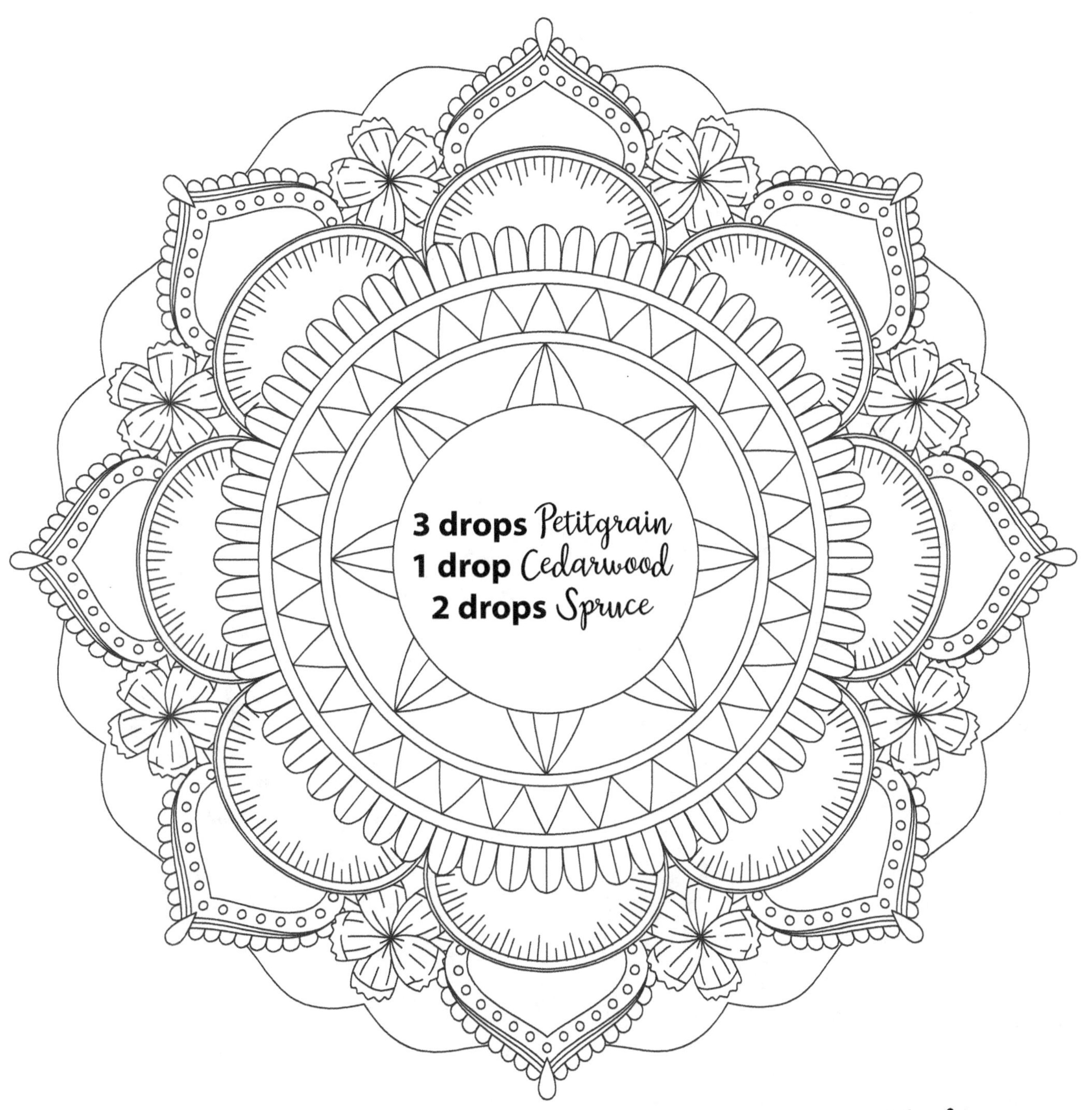

Meditation

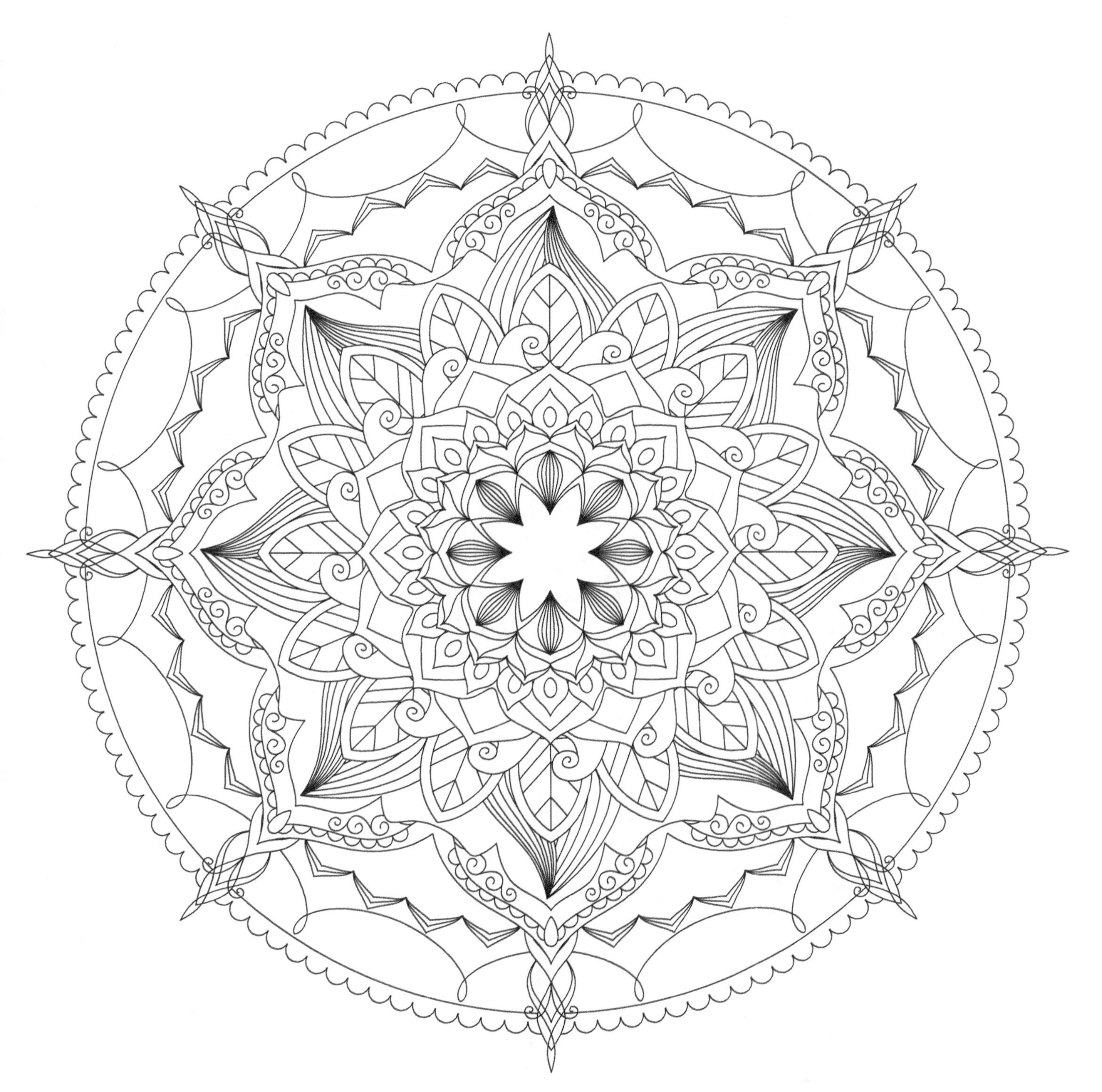

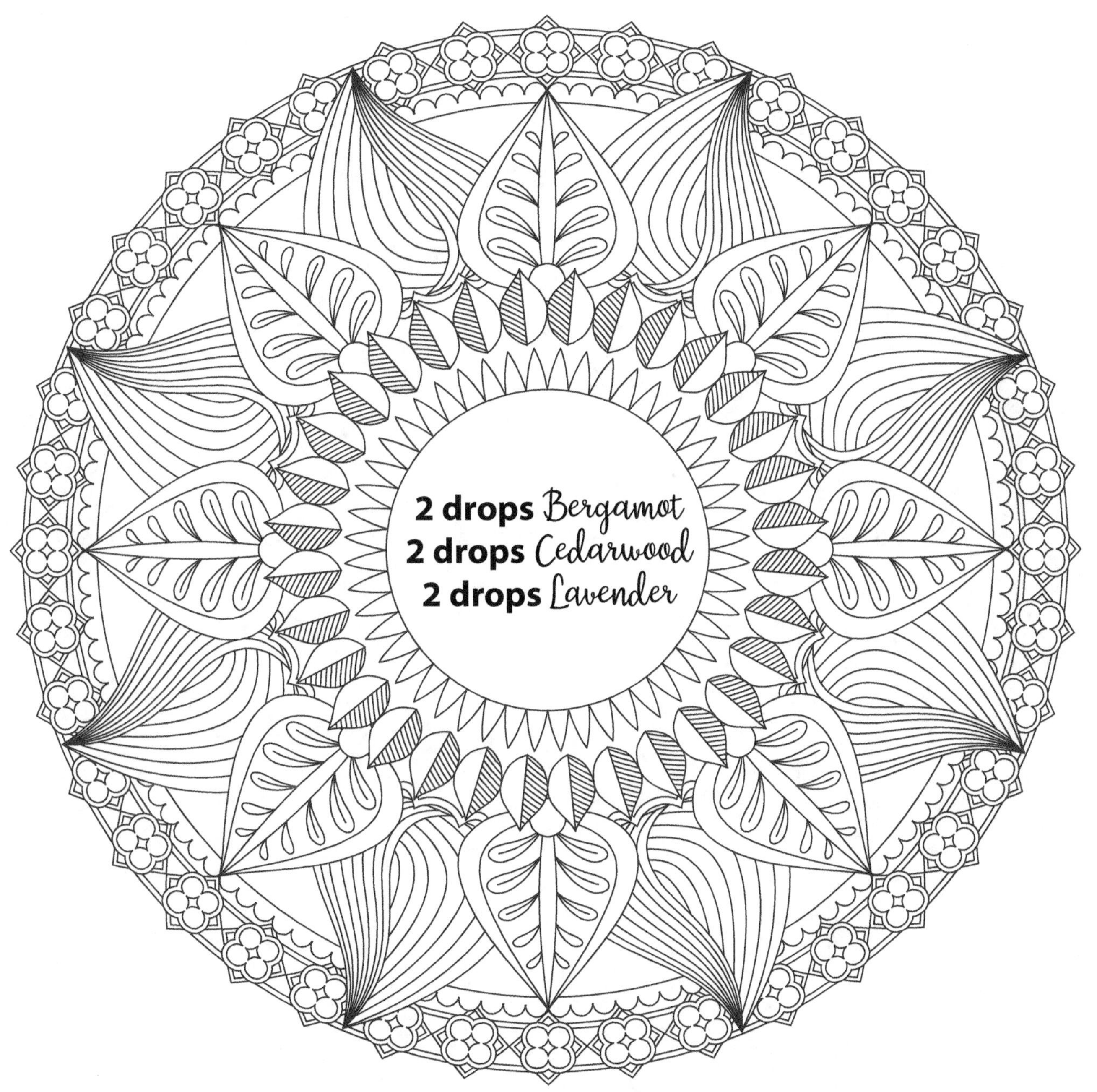

Focus

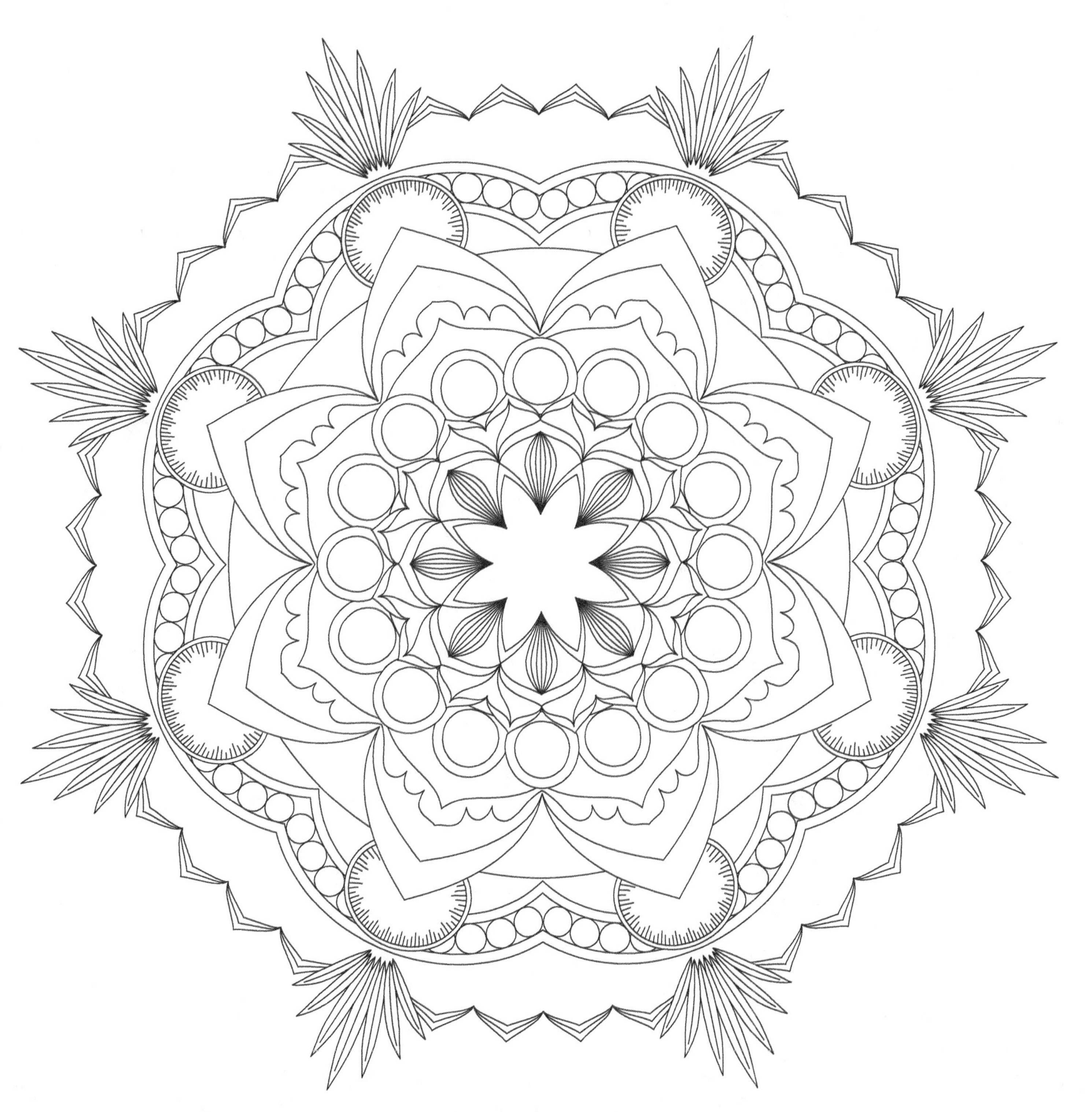

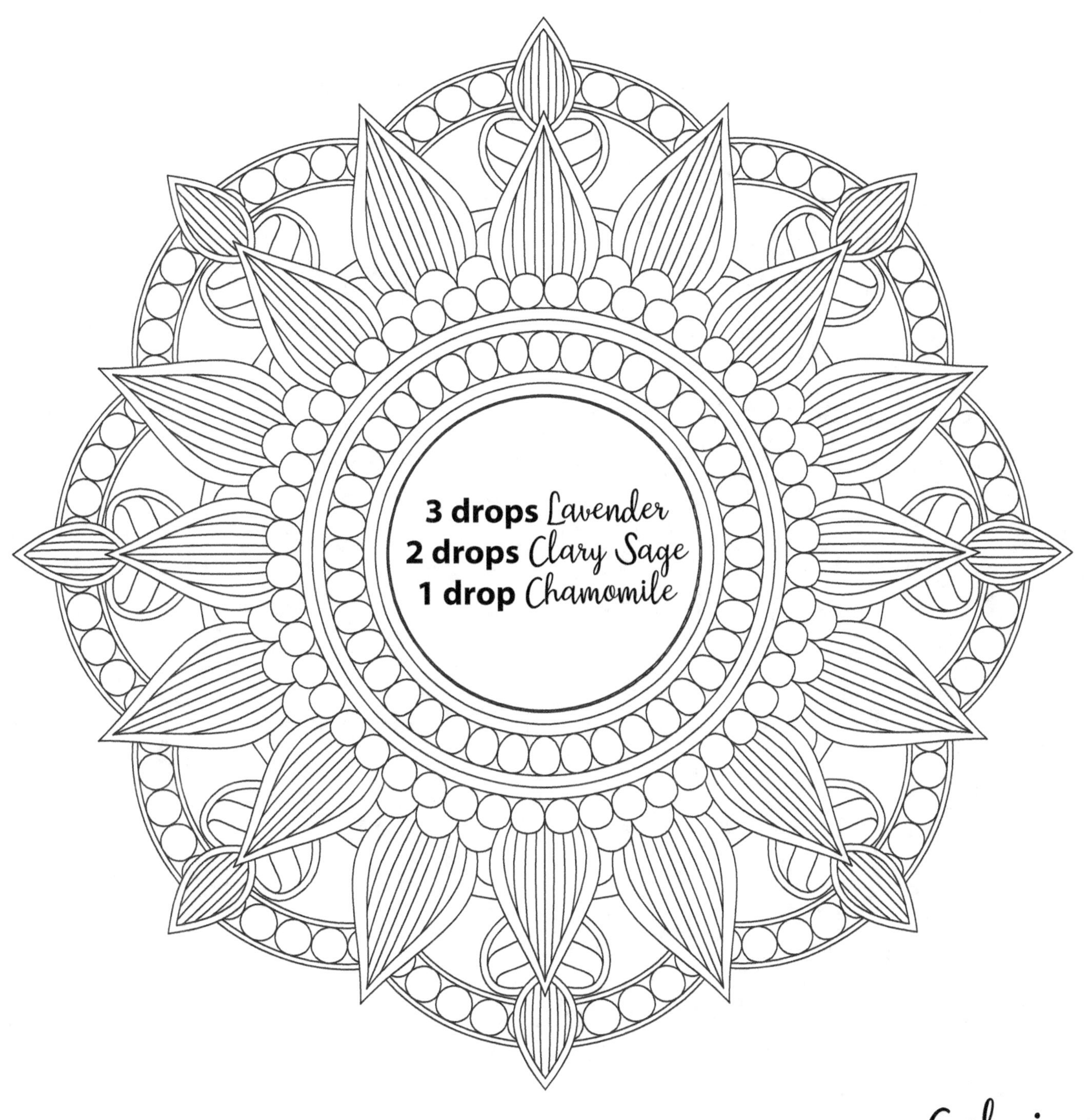

Calming

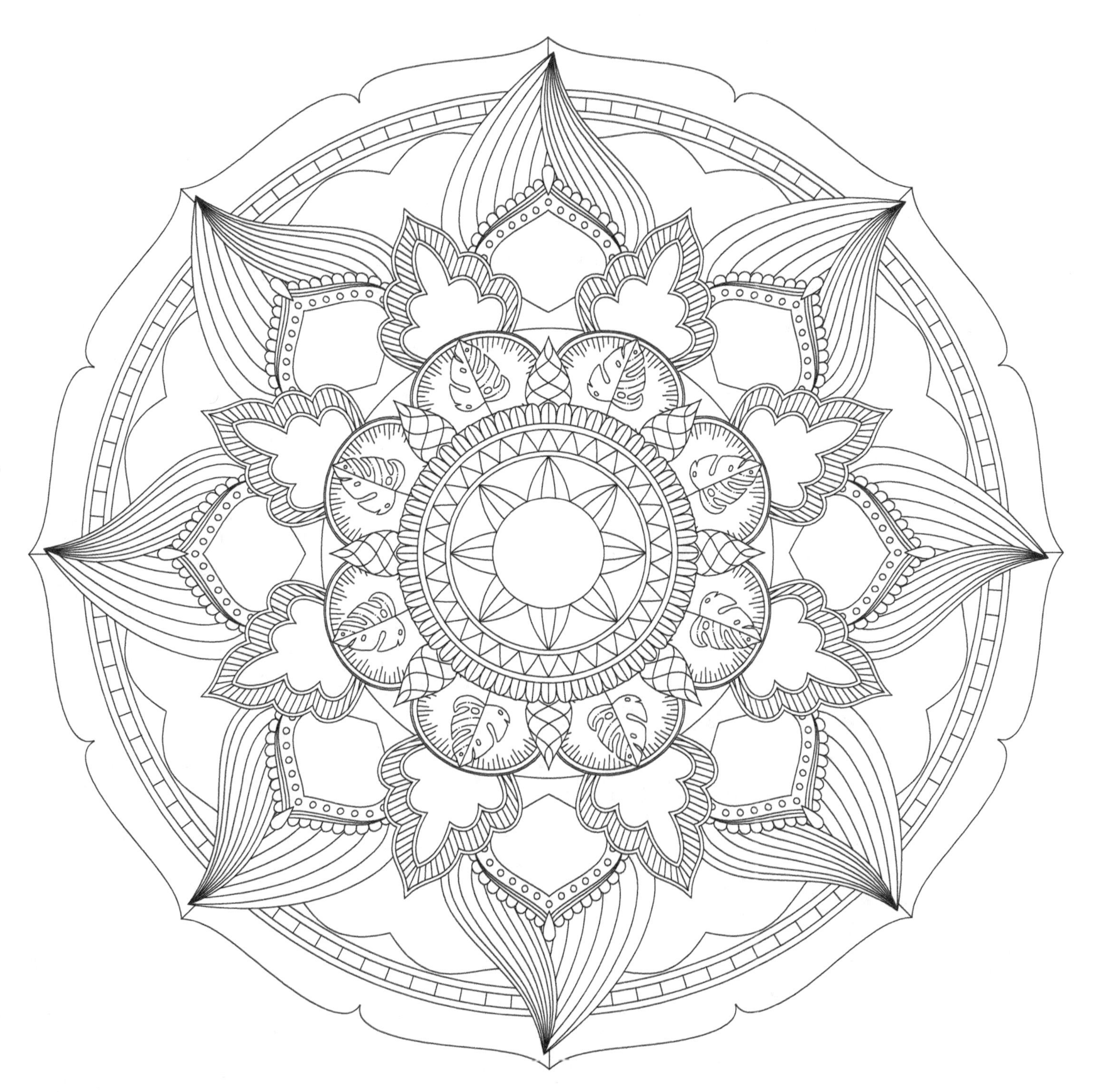

2 drops Lavender
2 drops Sweet Orange
1 drop Frankincense
1 drop Palo Santo

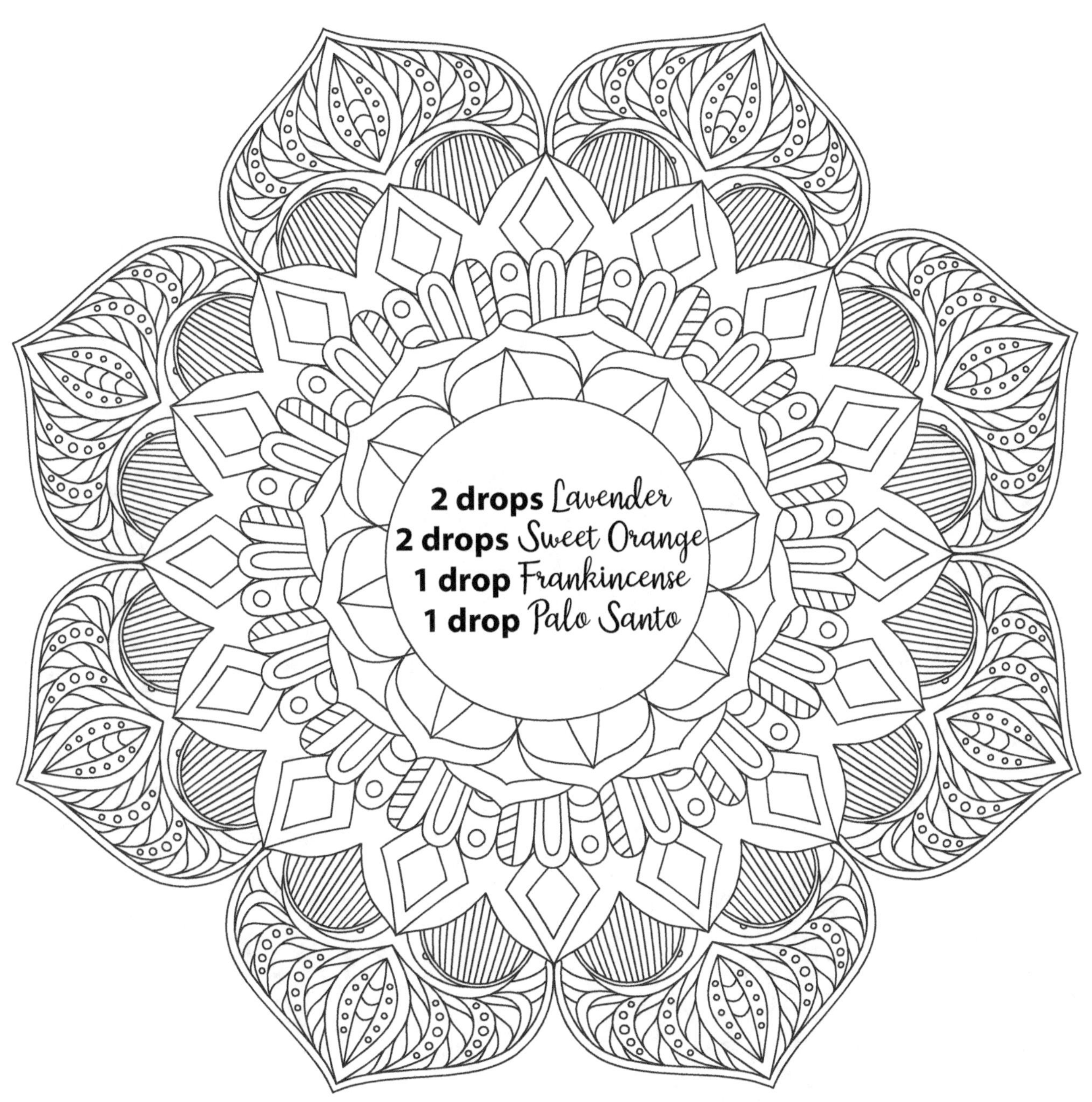

Grounding

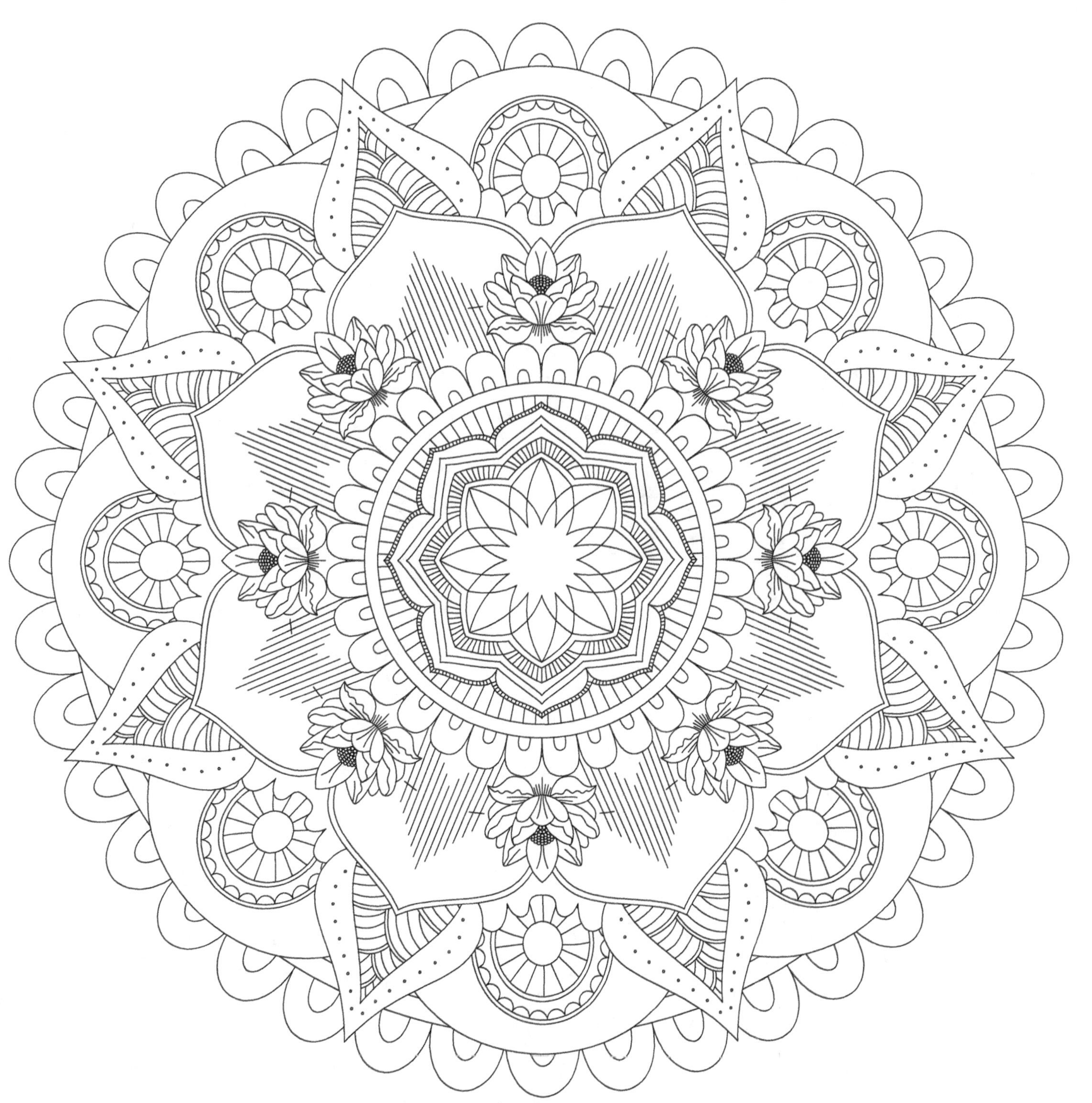

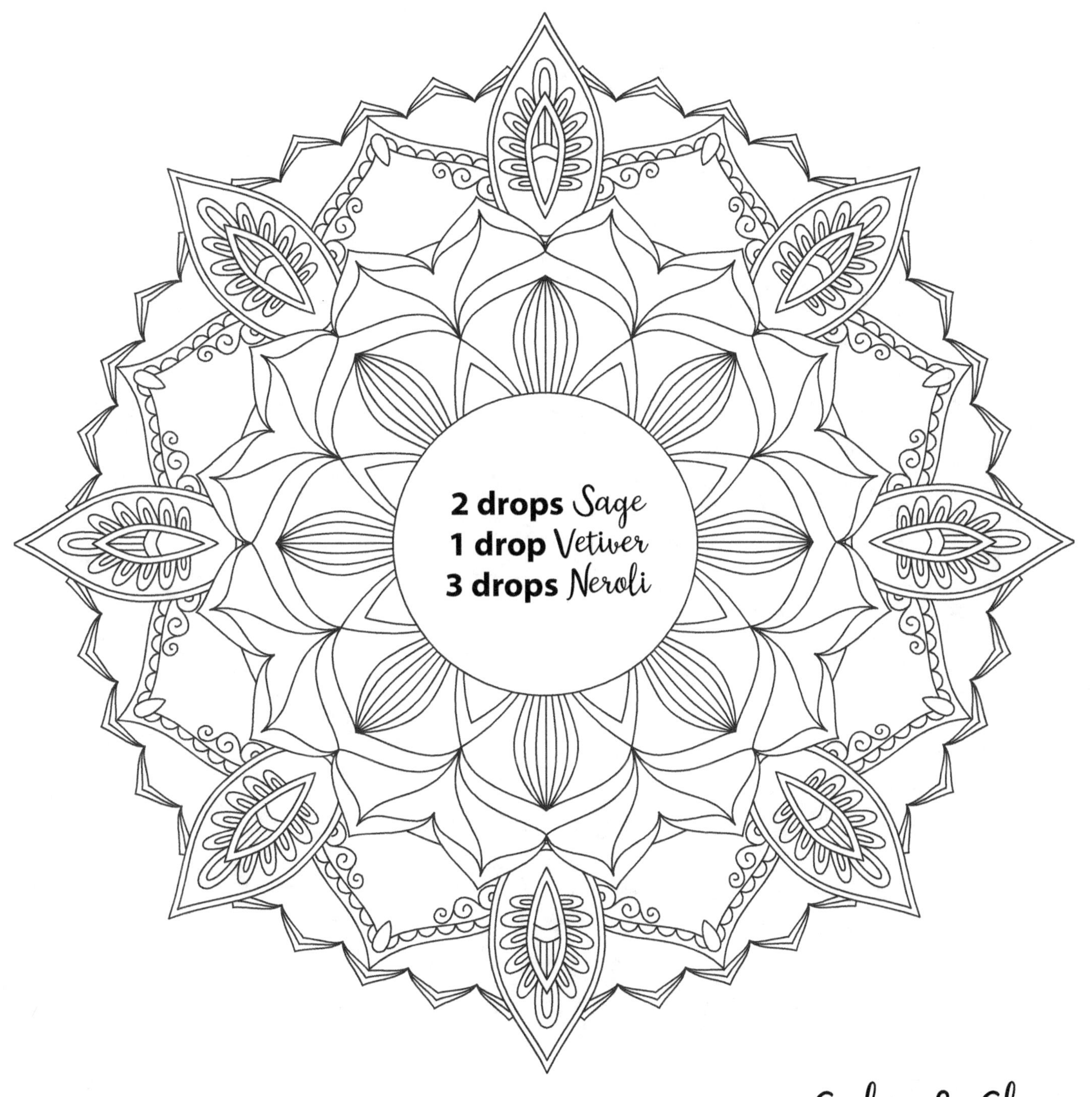

Calm & Clear

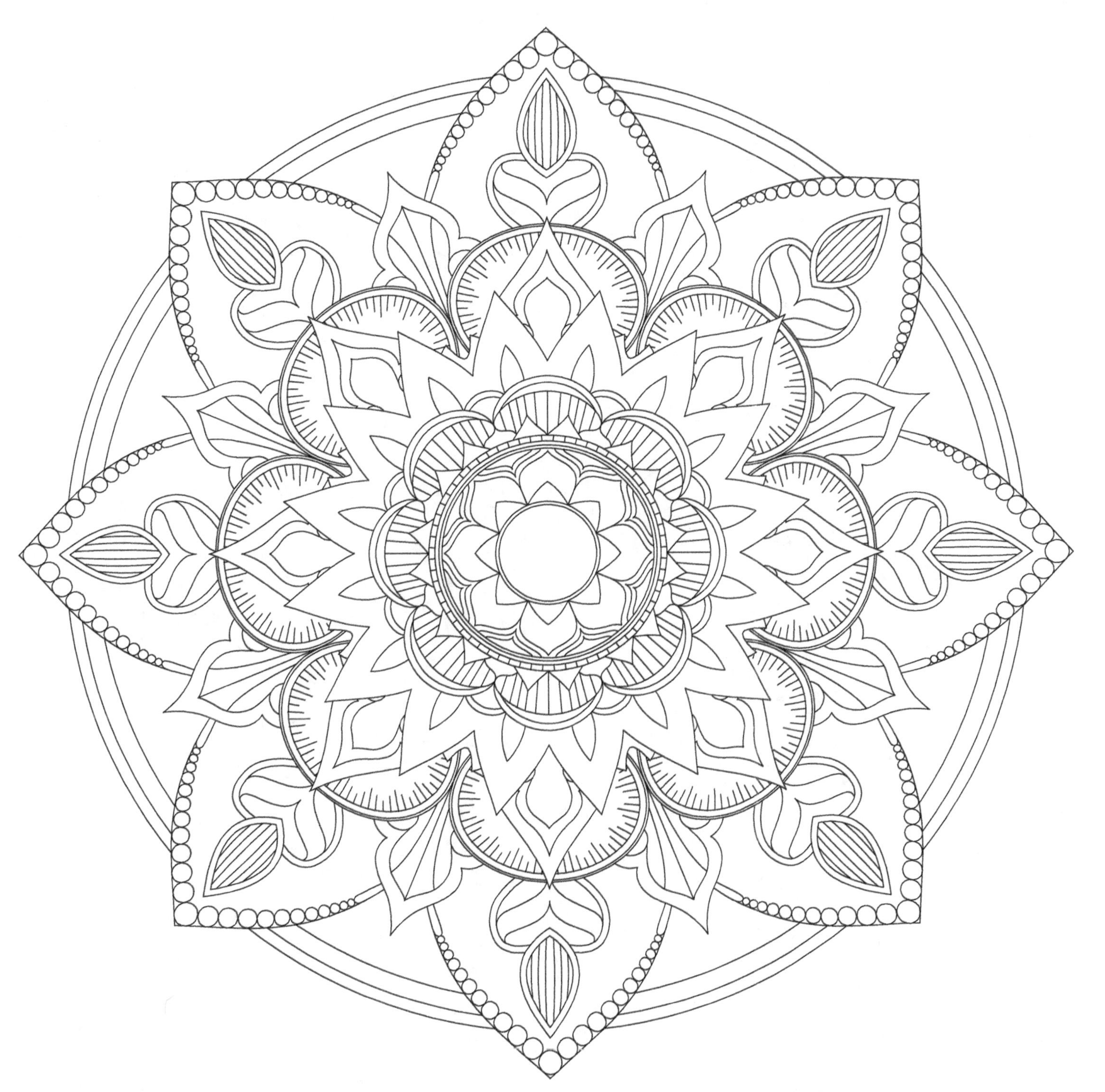

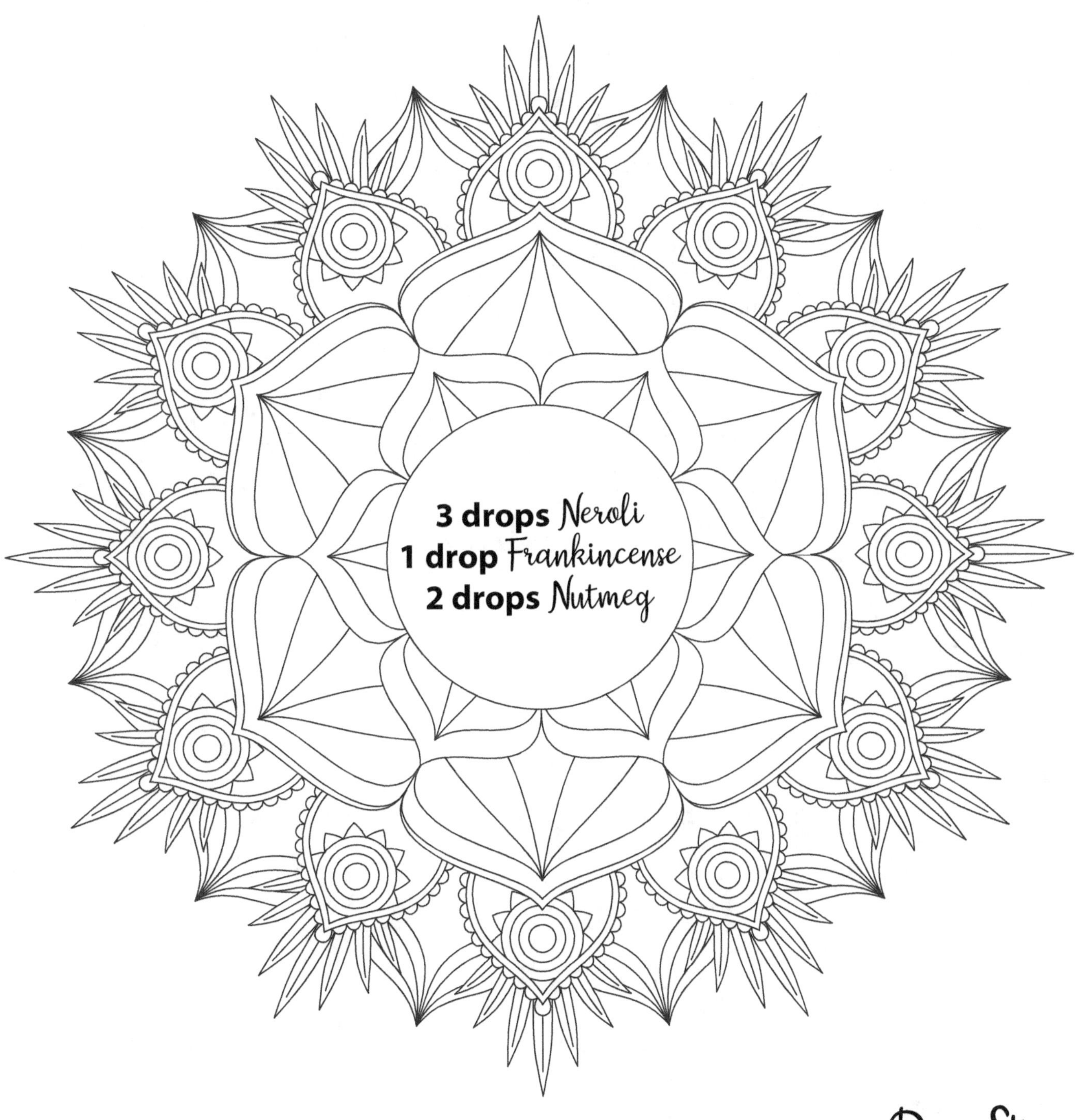

3 drops Neroli
1 drop Frankincense
2 drops Nutmeg
De-Stress

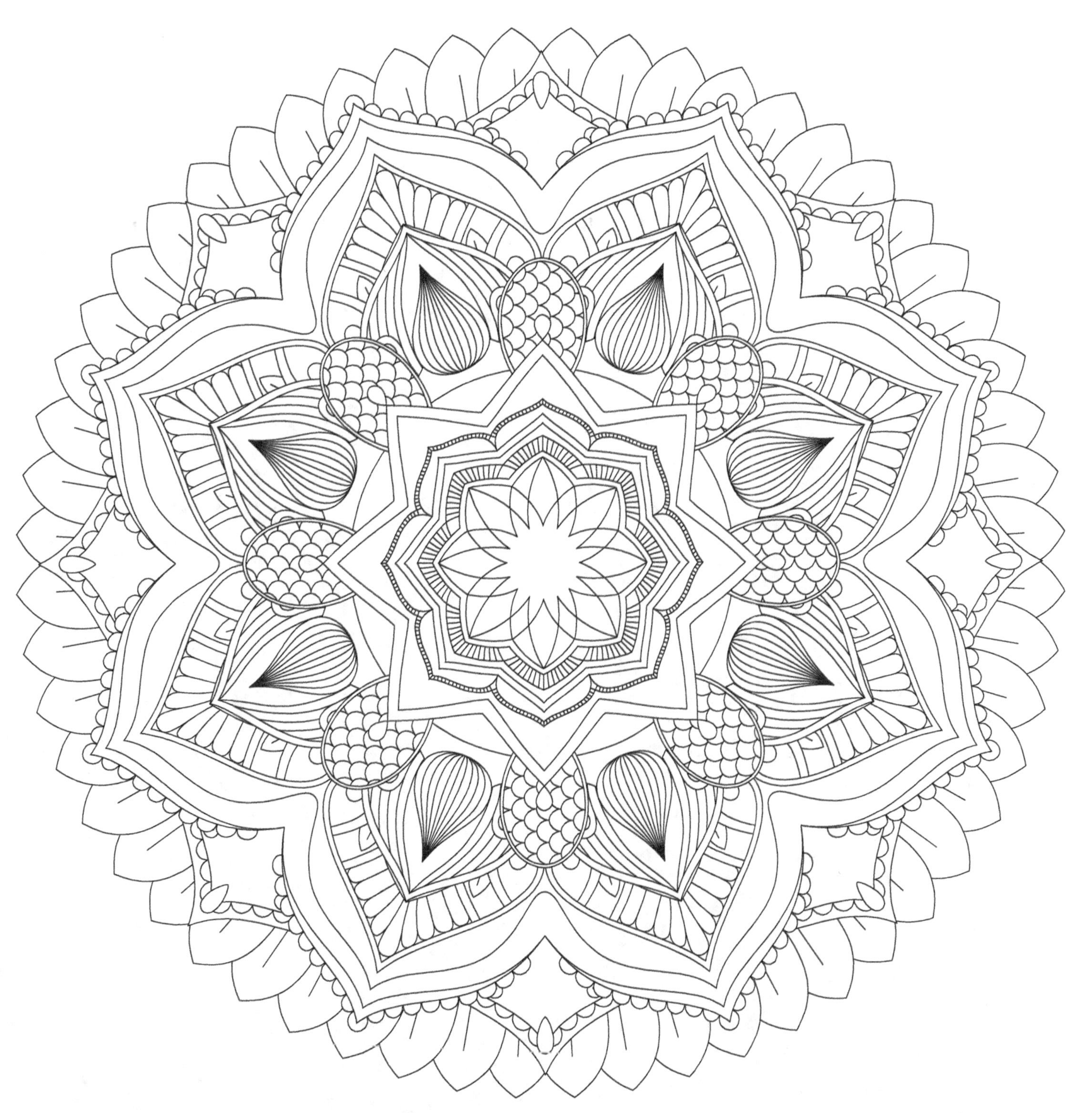

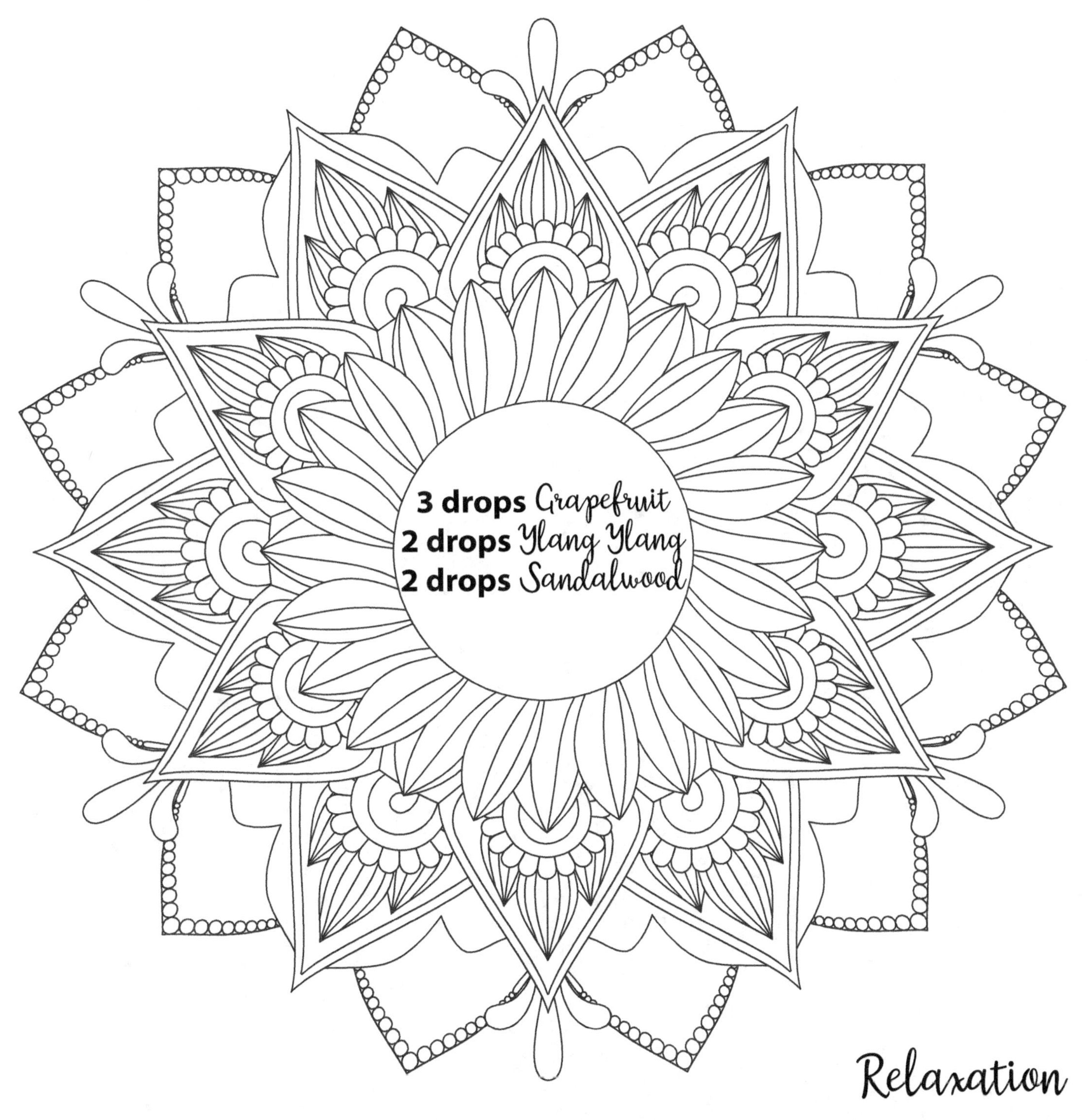

3 drops Grapefruit
2 drops Ylang Ylang
2 drops Sandalwood
Relaxation

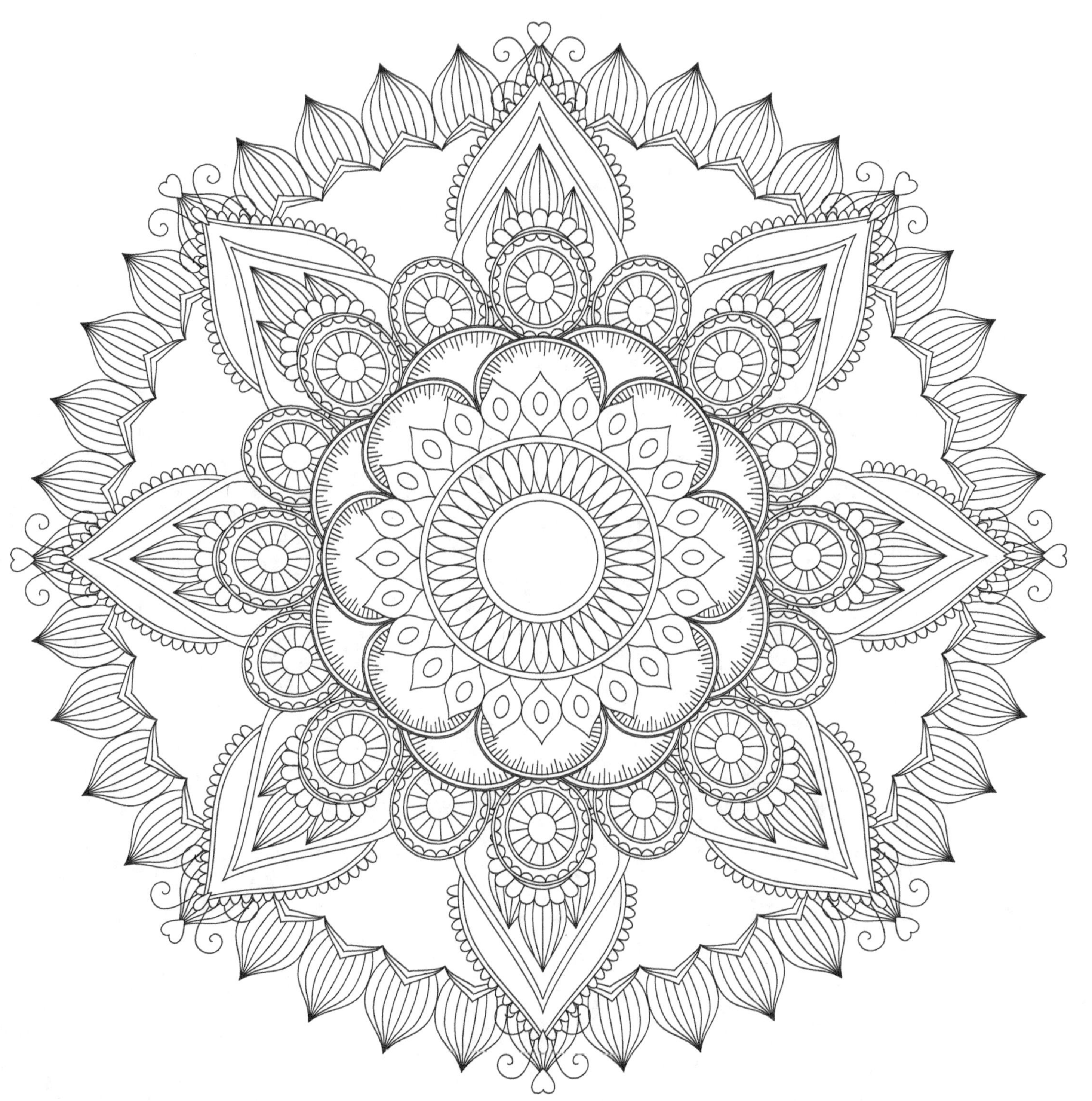

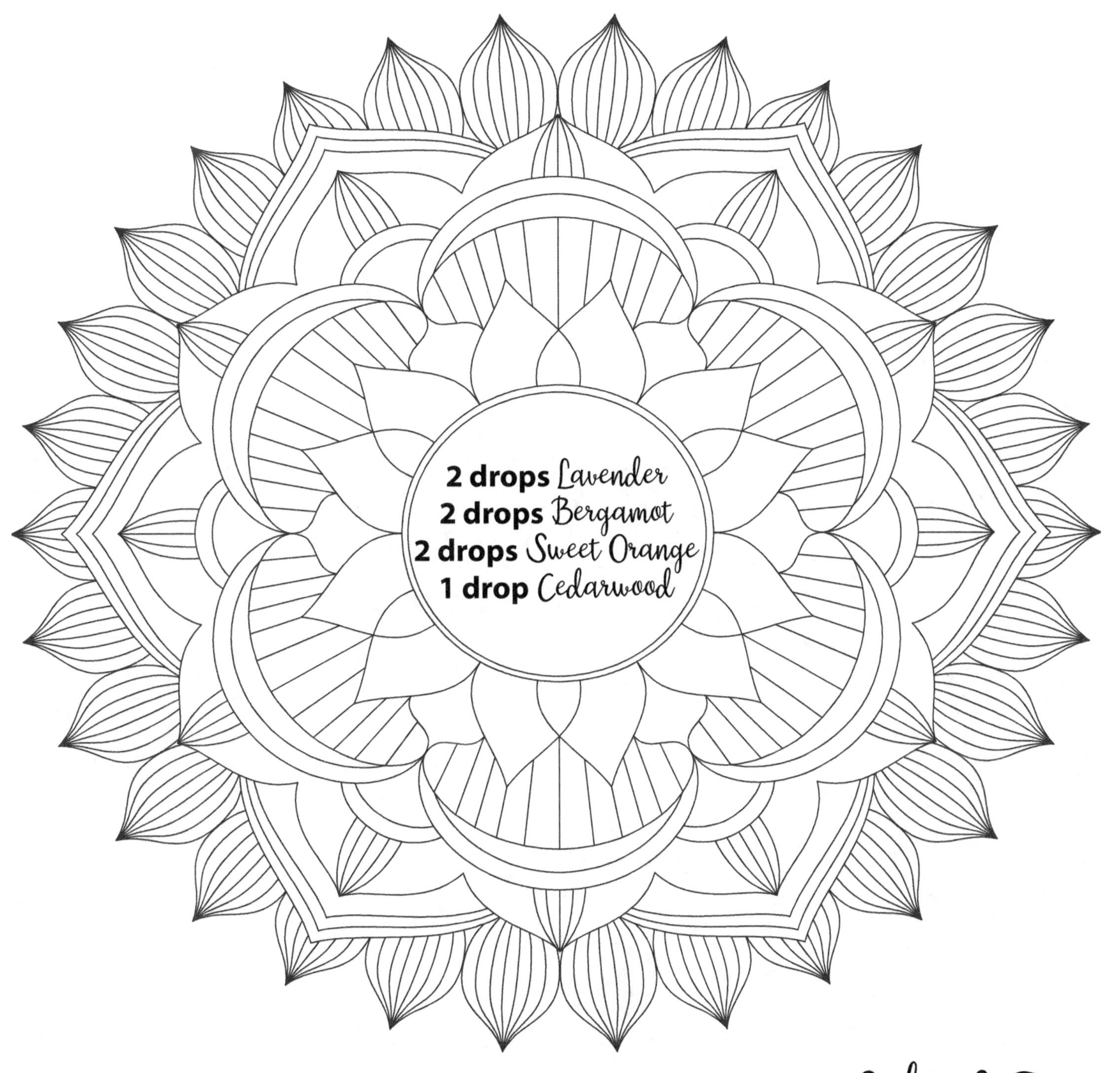

2 drops Lavender
2 drops Bergamot
2 drops Sweet Orange
1 drop Cedarwood
Calm & Zen

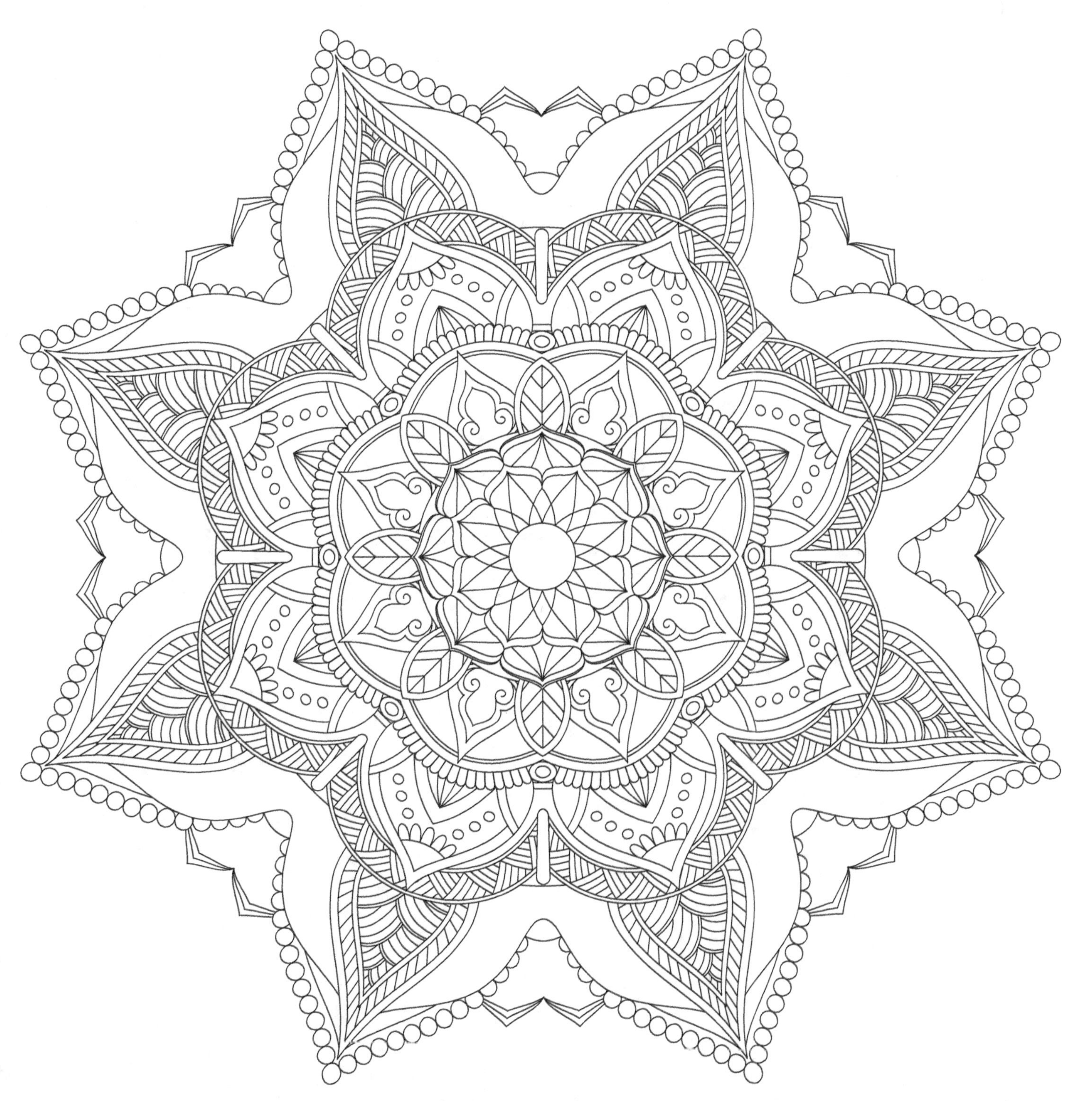

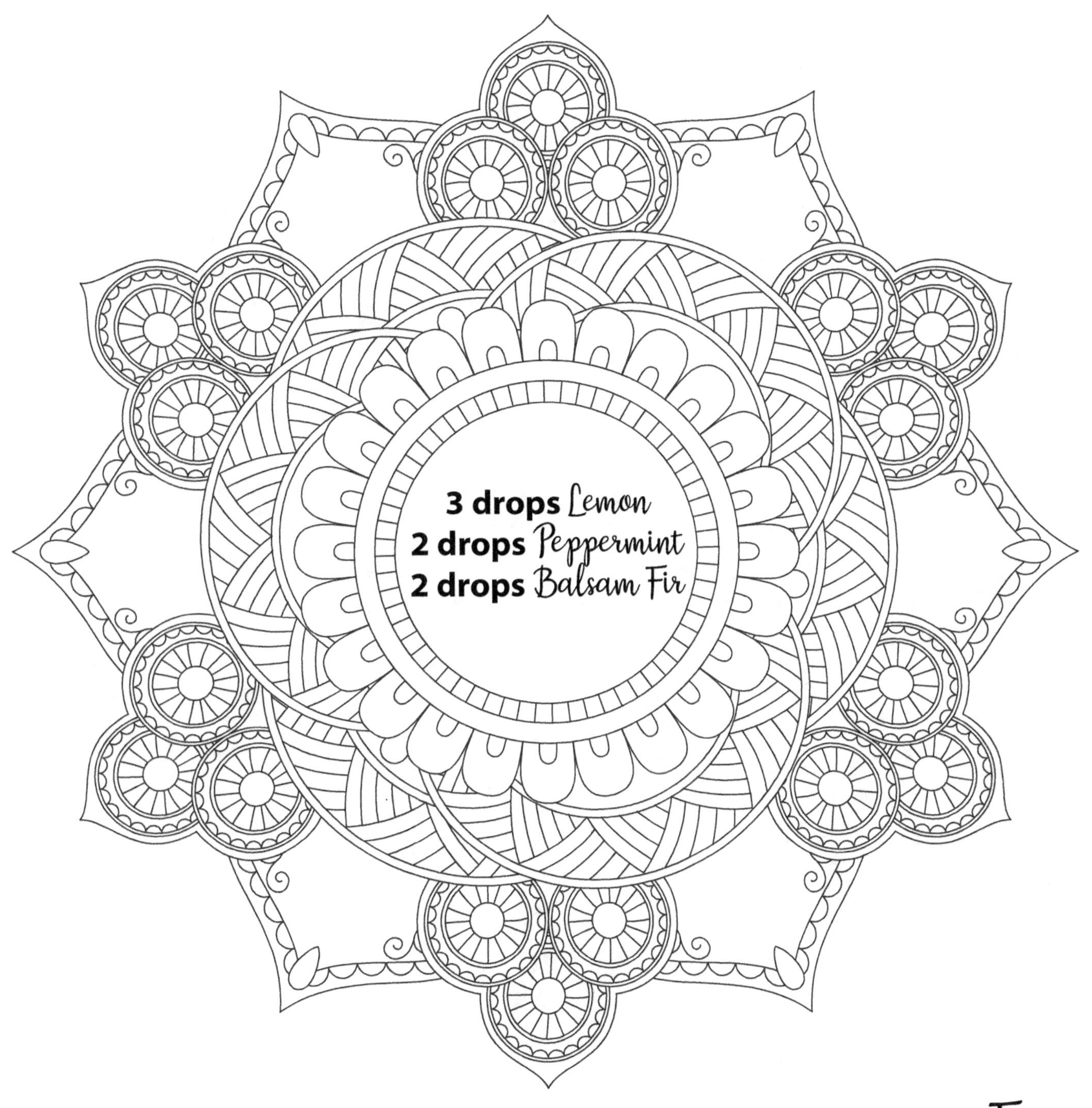

3 drops Lemon
2 drops Peppermint
2 drops Balsam Fir
Focus

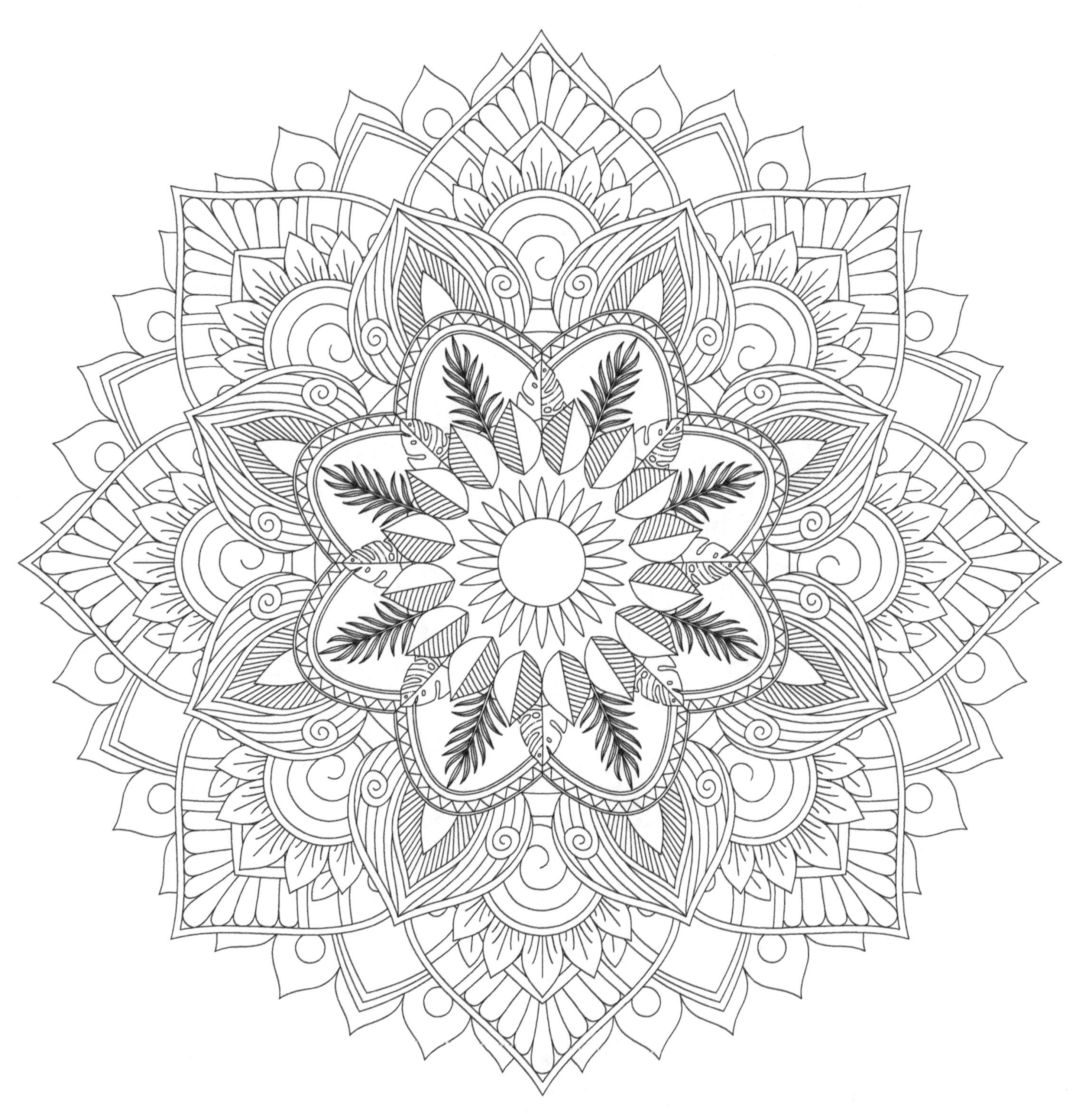

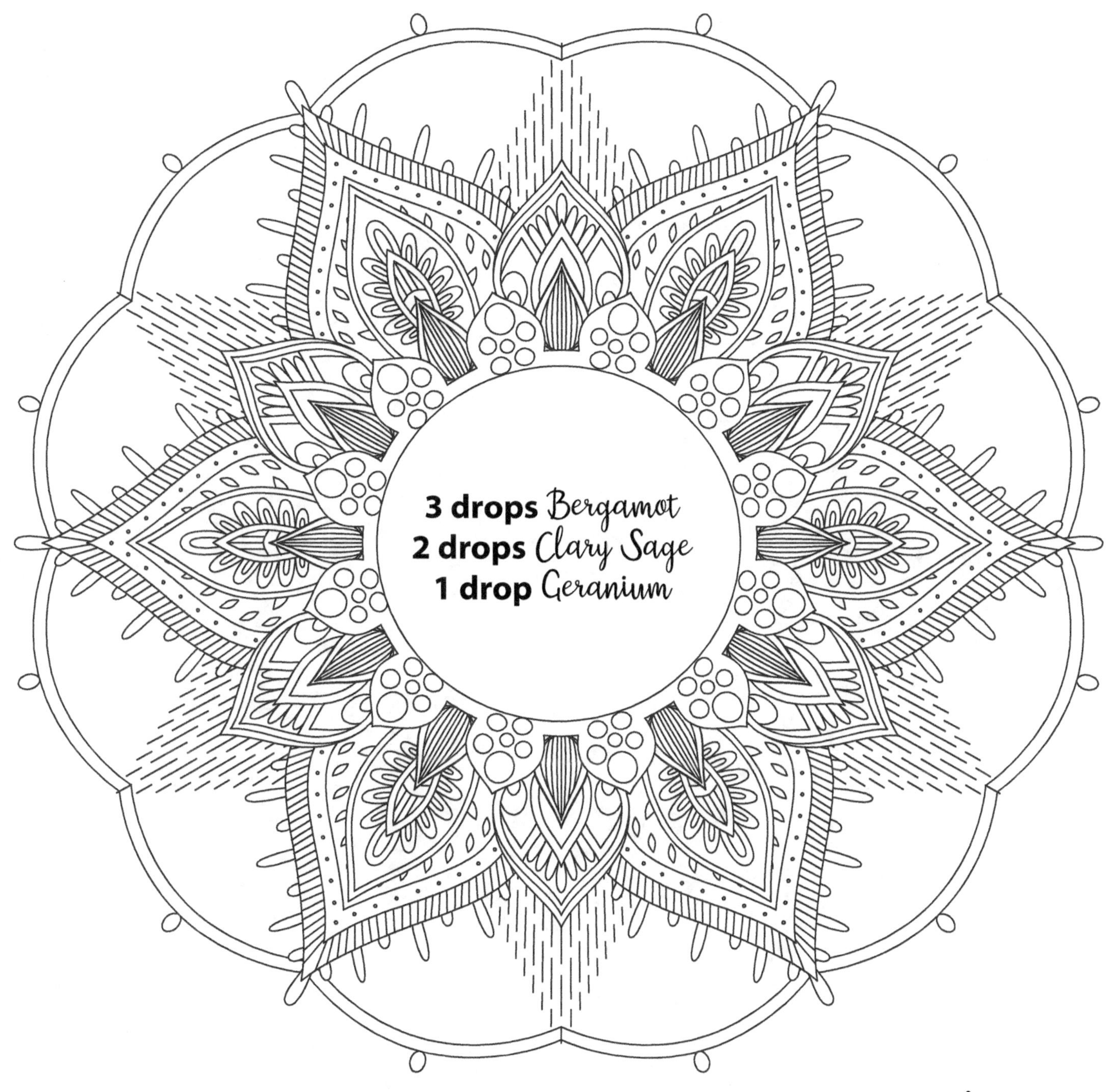

3 drops Bergamot
2 drops Clary Sage
1 drop Geranium
Anxious

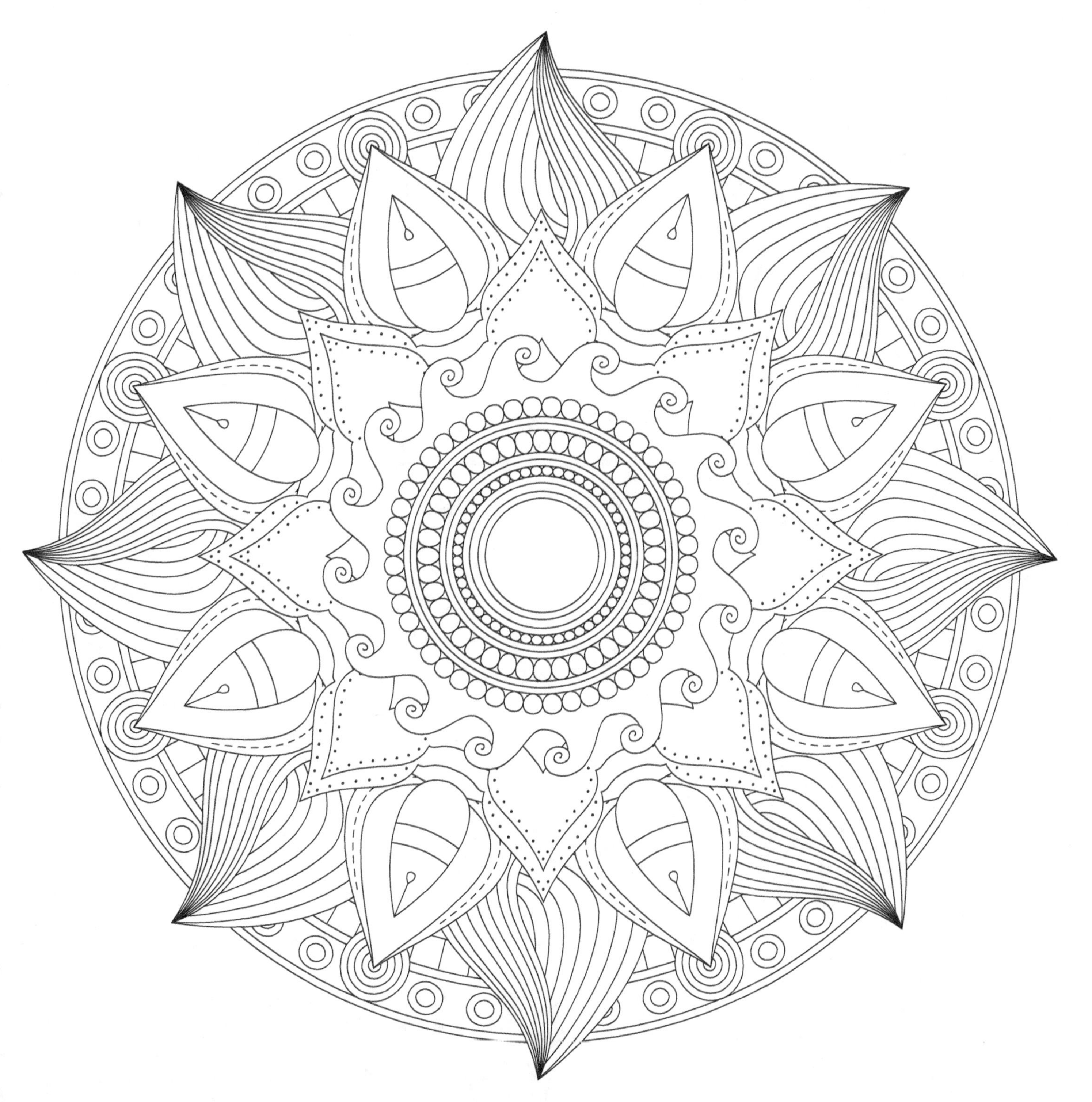

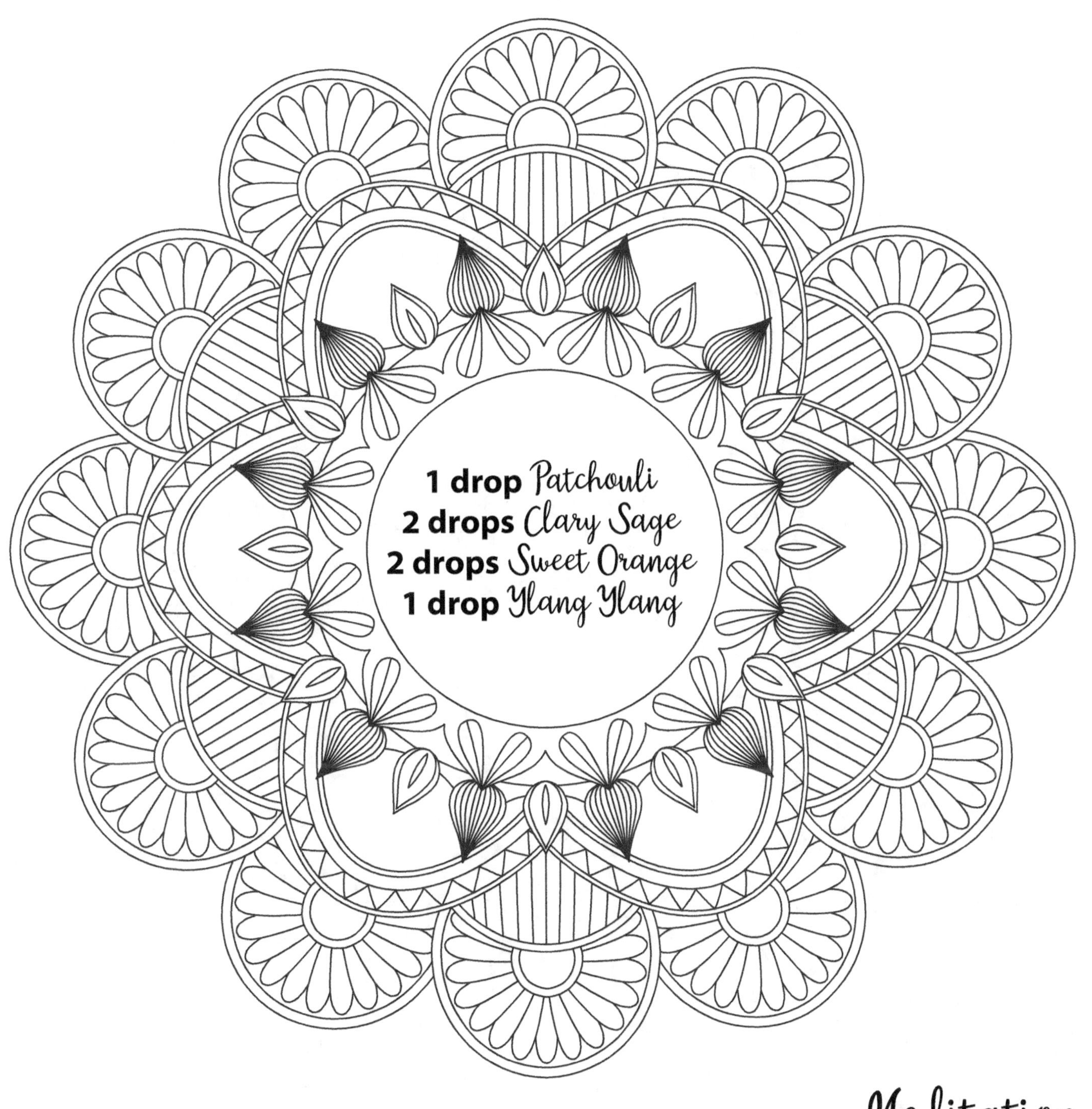

1 drop Patchouli
2 drops Clary Sage
2 drops Sweet Orange
1 drop Ylang Ylang
Meditation

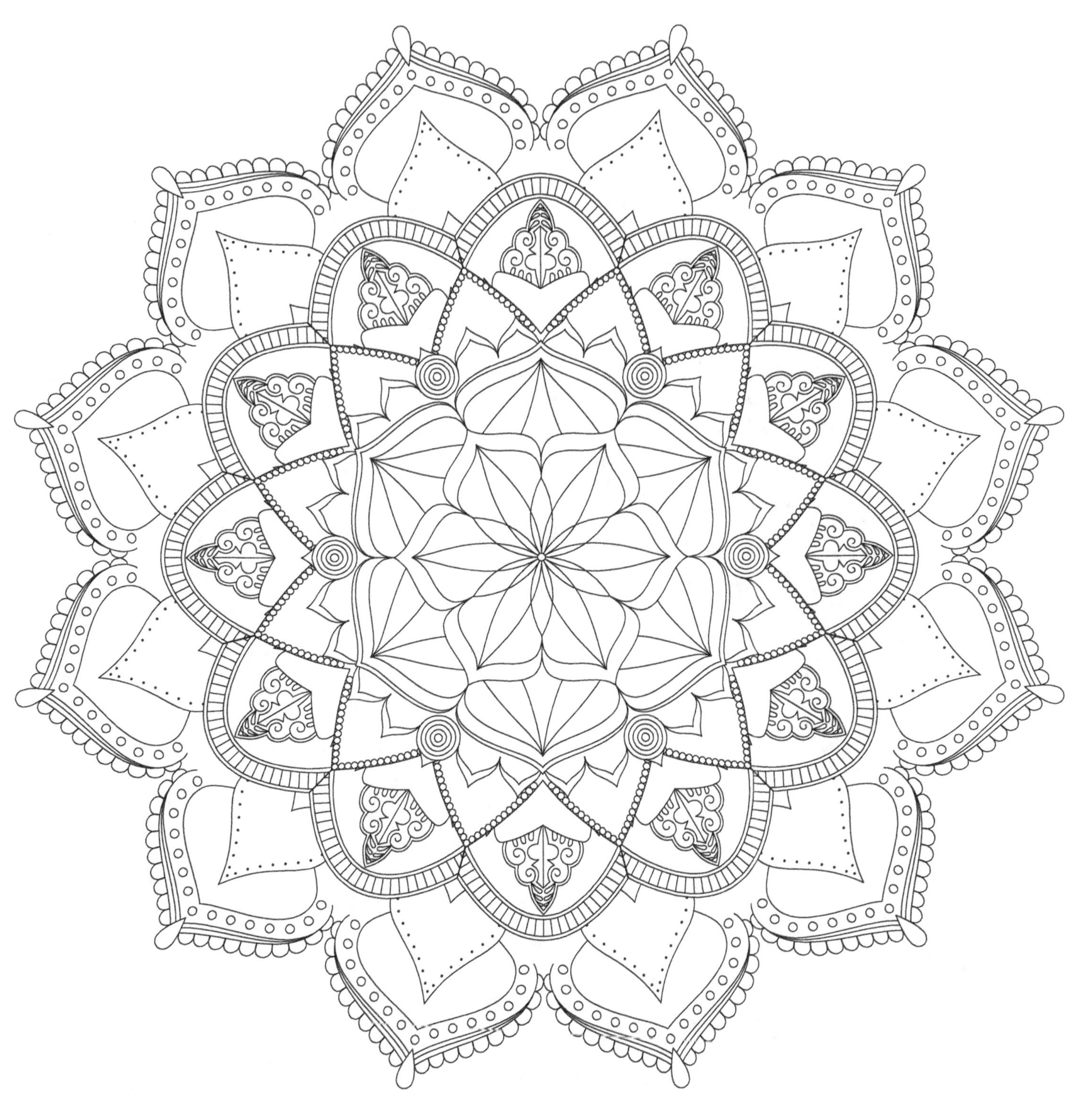

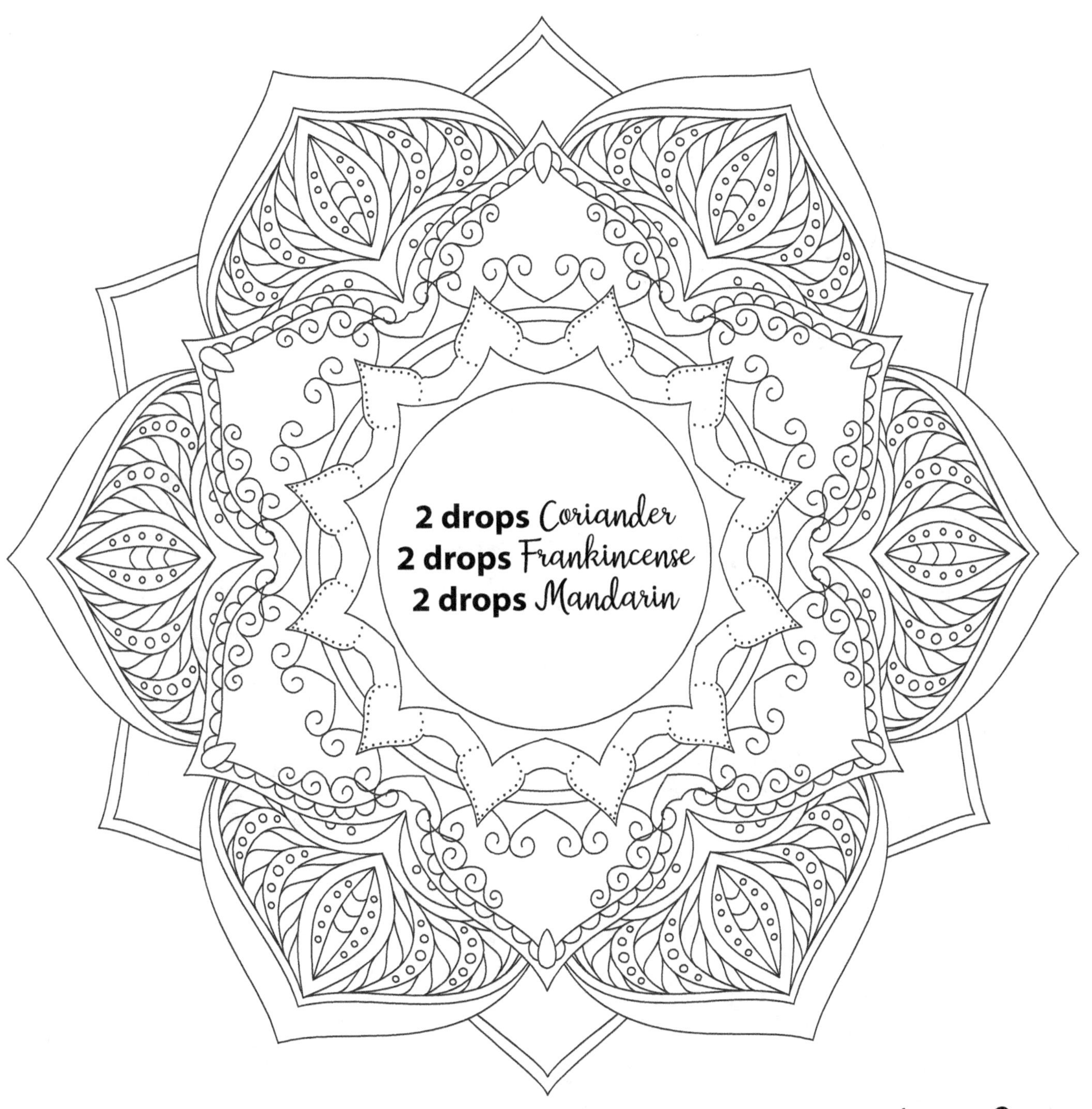

2 drops Coriander
2 drops Frankincense
2 drops Mandarin
De-Stress

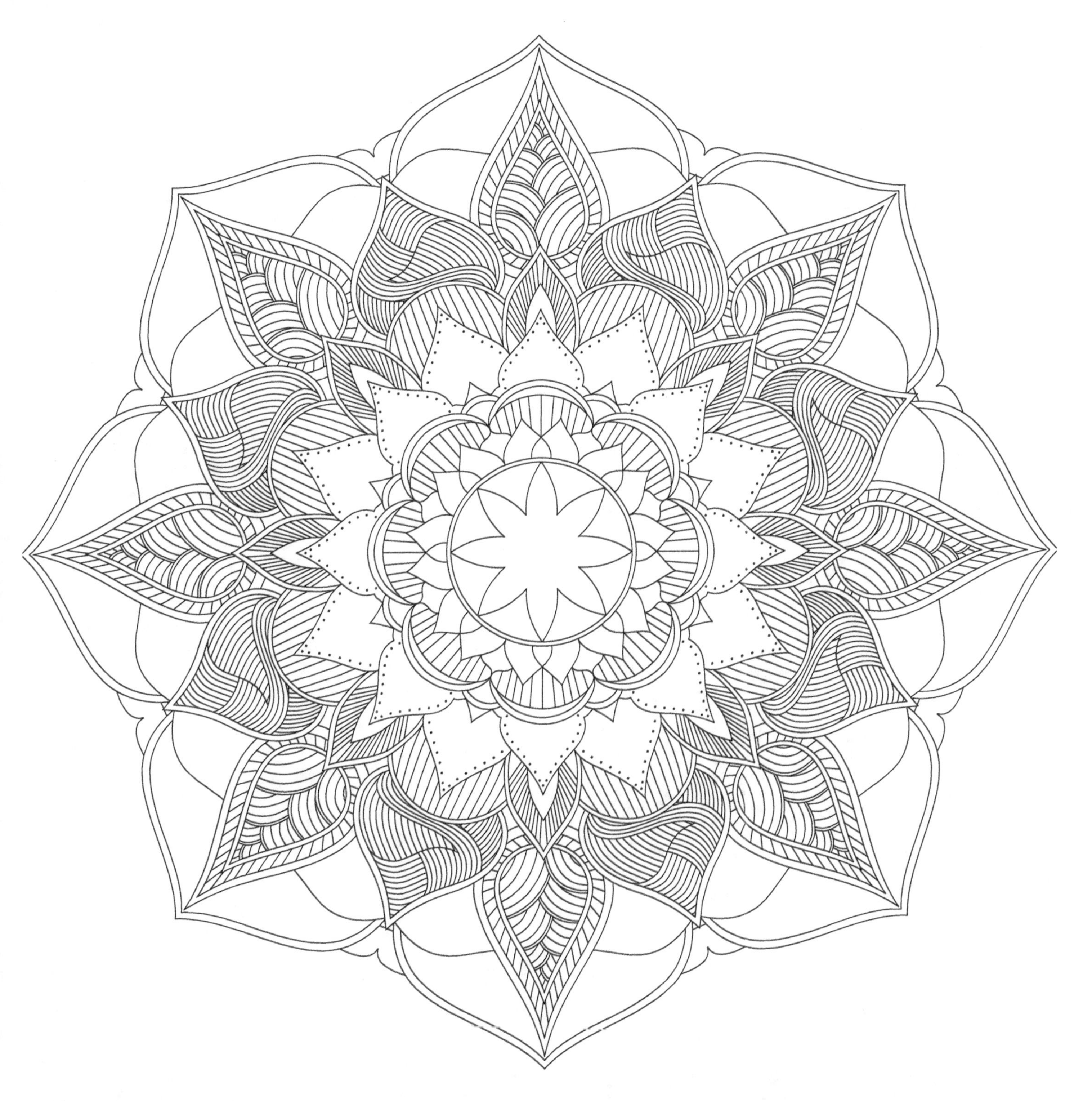

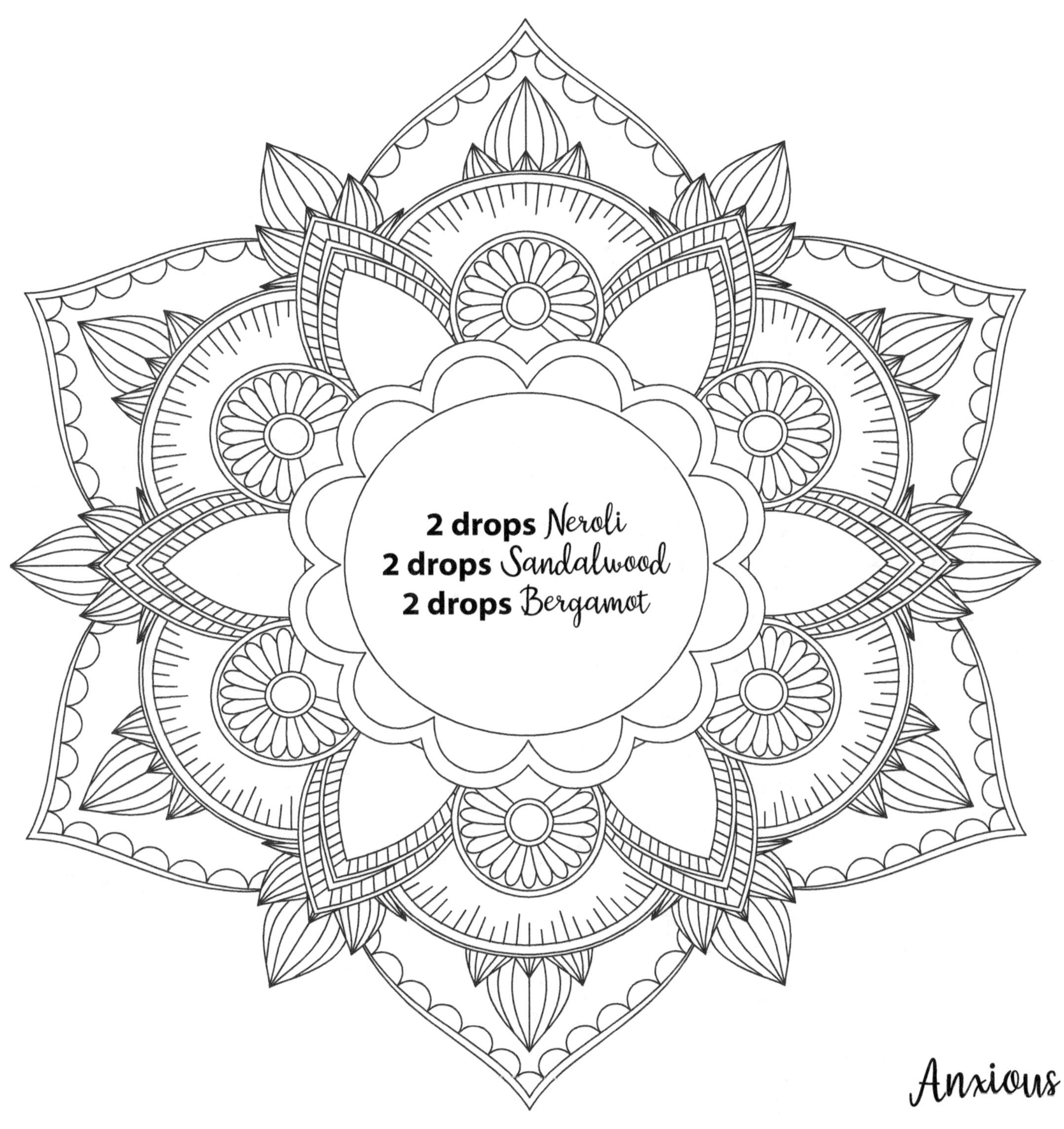

2 drops Neroli
2 drops Sandalwood
2 drops Bergamot
Anxious

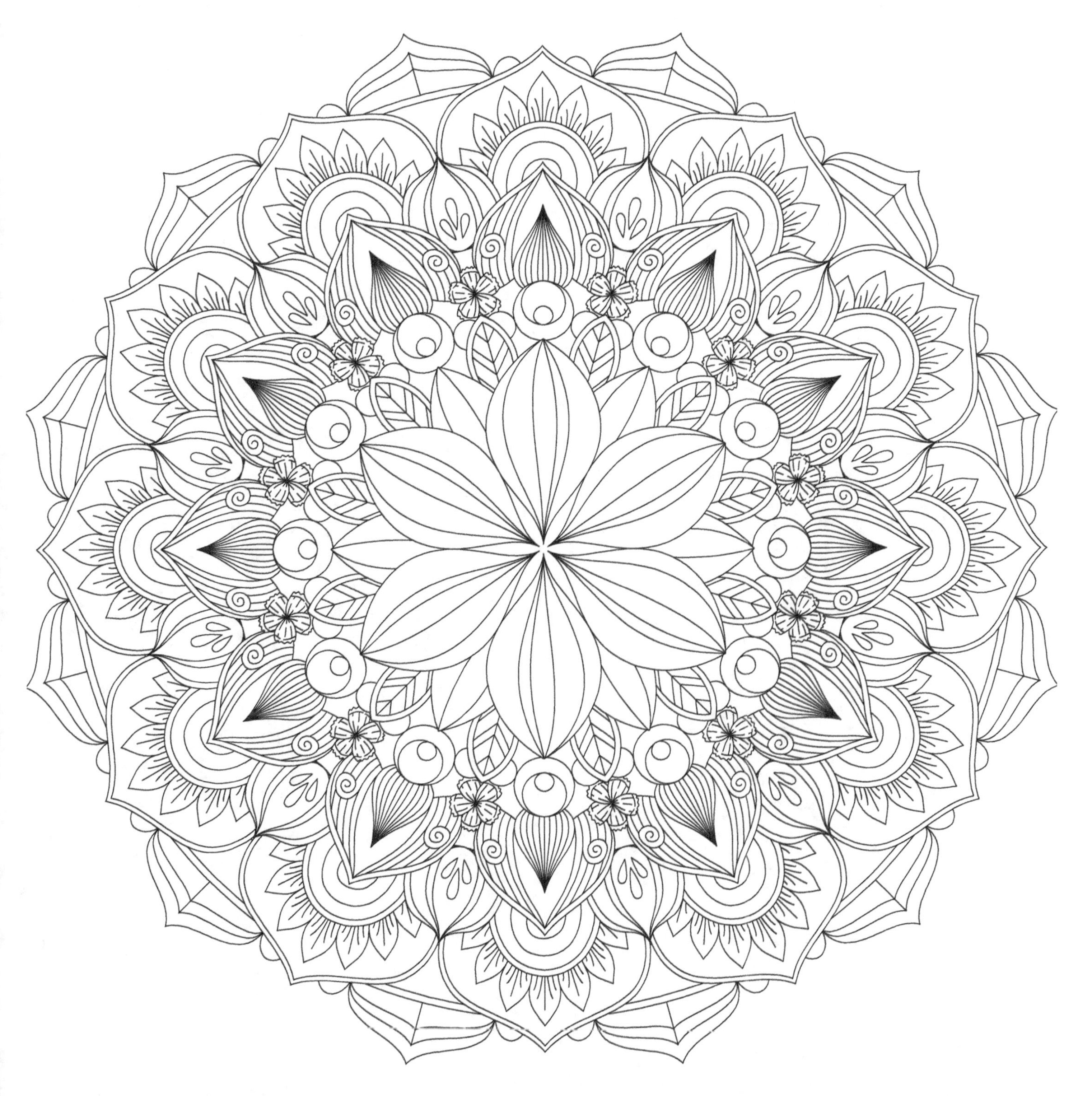

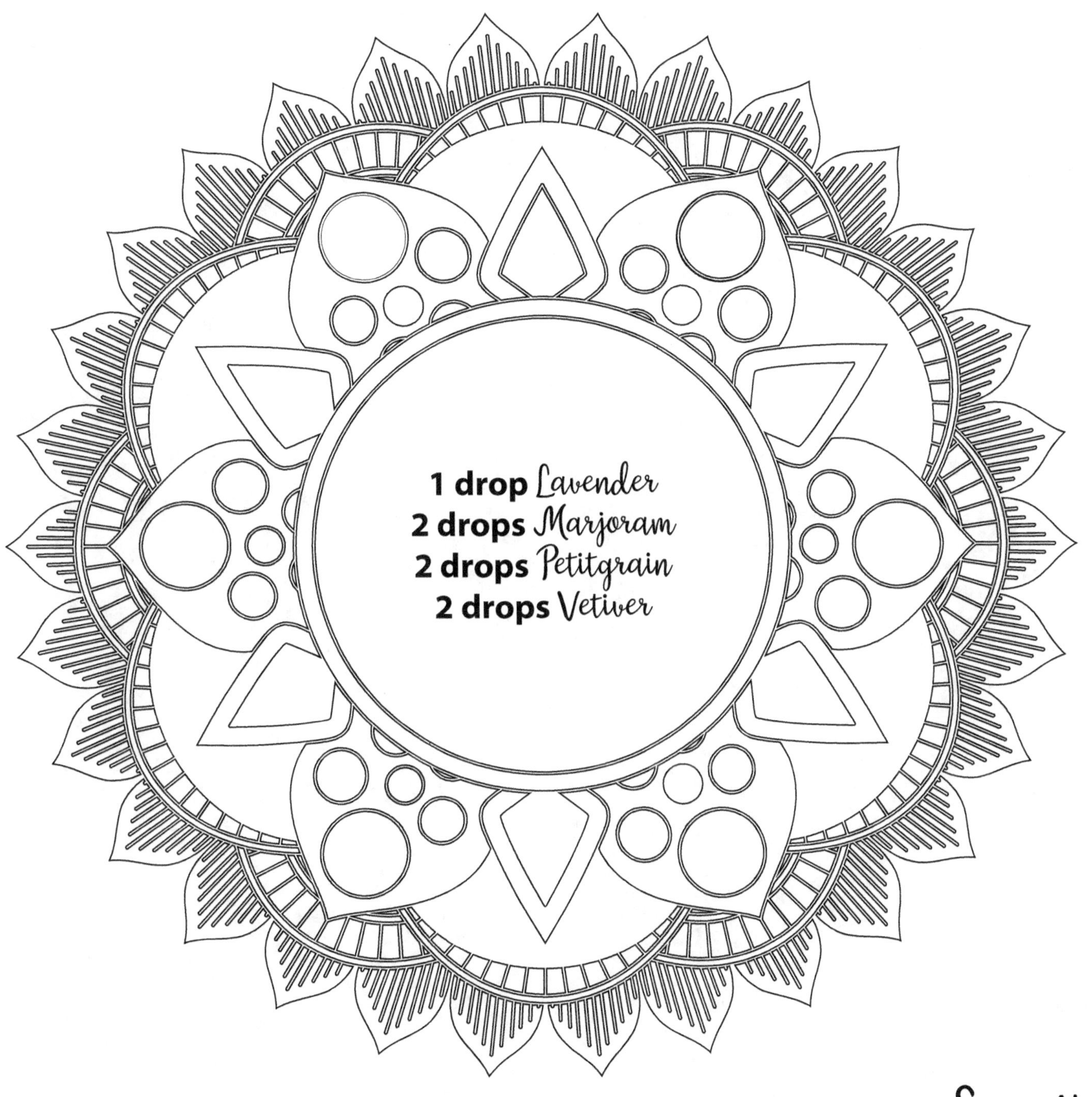

1 drop Lavender
2 drops Marjoram
2 drops Petitgrain
2 drops Vetiver
Serenity

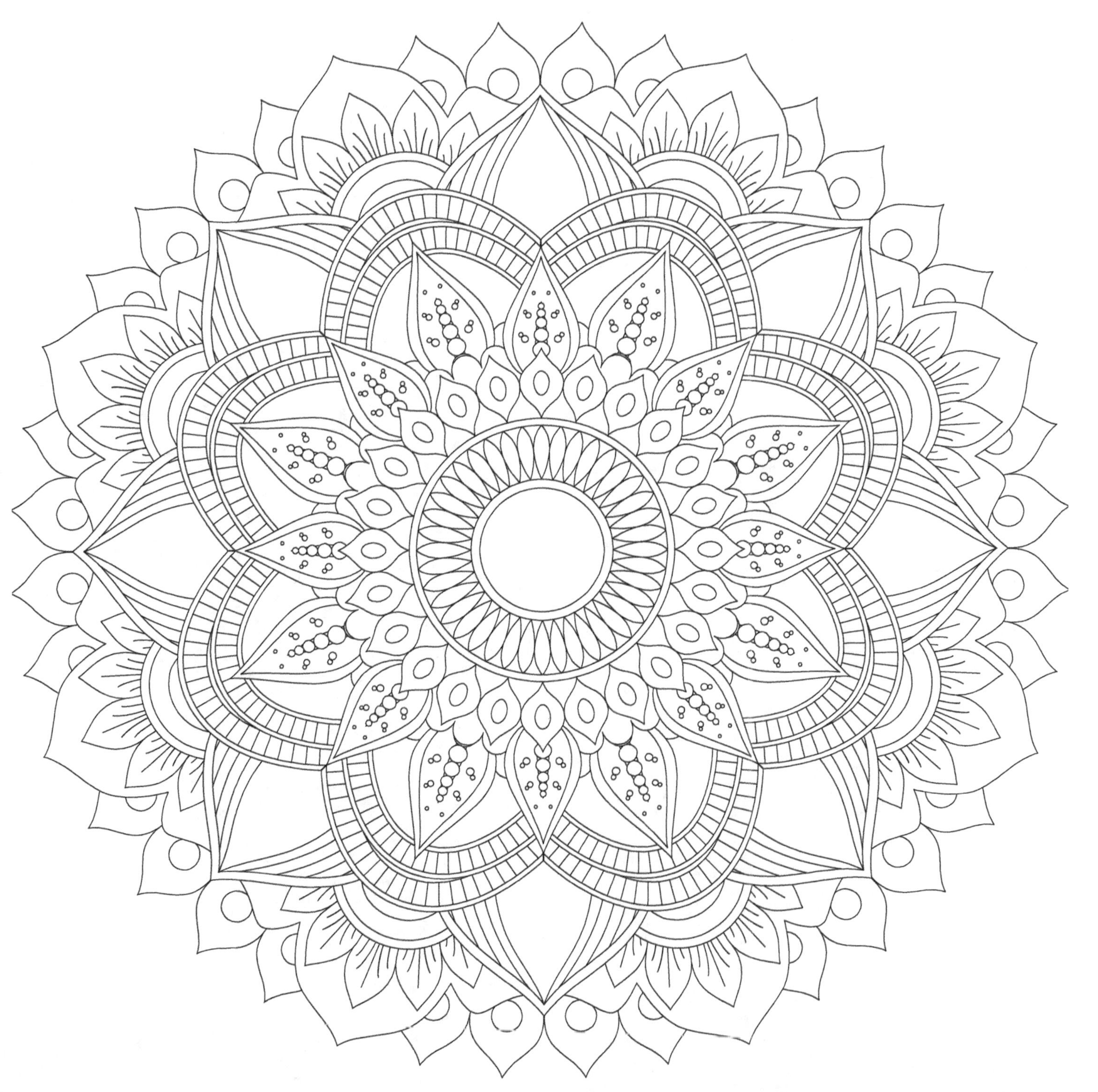

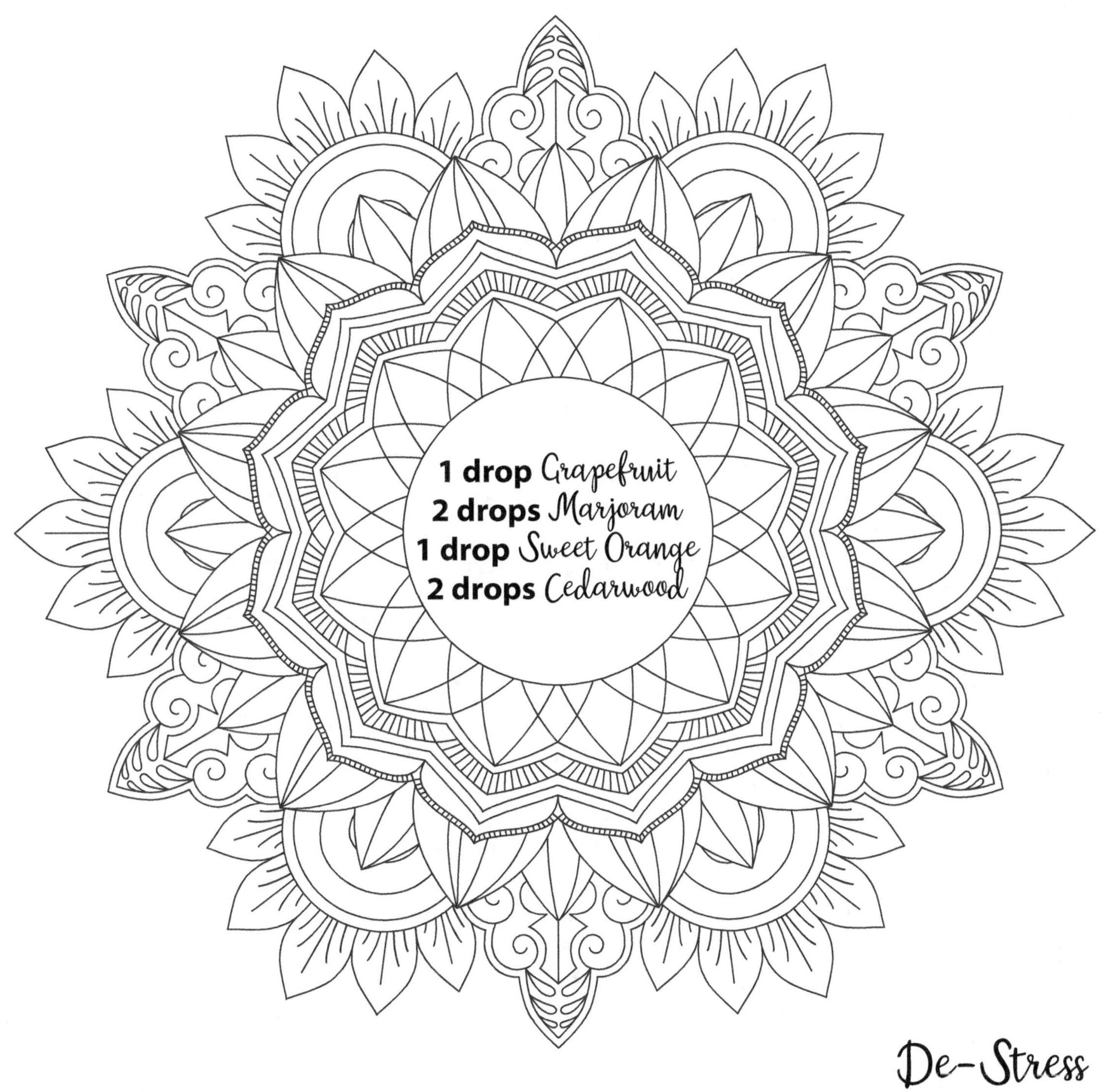

1 drop Grapefruit
2 drops Marjoram
1 drop Sweet Orange
2 drops Cedarwood
De-Stress

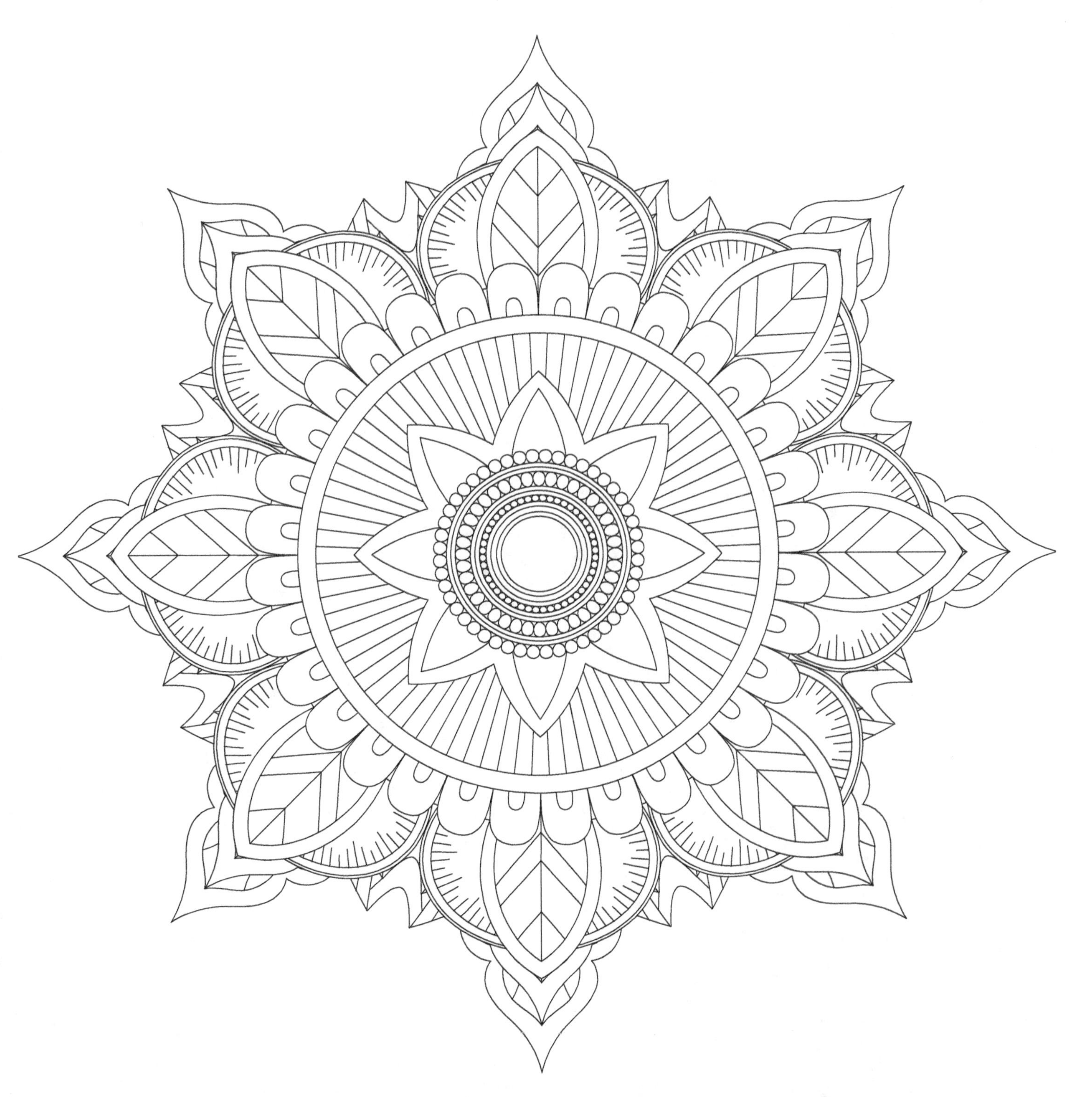

Other Books from Escentual Web

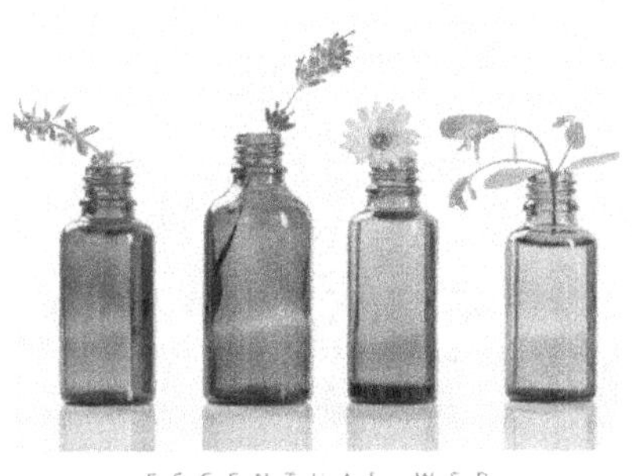

Want to make blends but not sure where to start? This book is written for the home user who just wants a simple process to follow.

Not sure which oils to use for each complaint? Use the 50+ included tables for skin, emotional, and physical conditions, thoroughly researched from over a dozen sources.

Includes:
*   Space to record 80 of your creations--never forget a winning blend again.
*   Reference tables for common carrier oils, dilution guidelines, and a safety cheat sheet for the most common essential oils, including which need to be used in low dilutions.
*   All the information you need to create and record your blends in one spot.

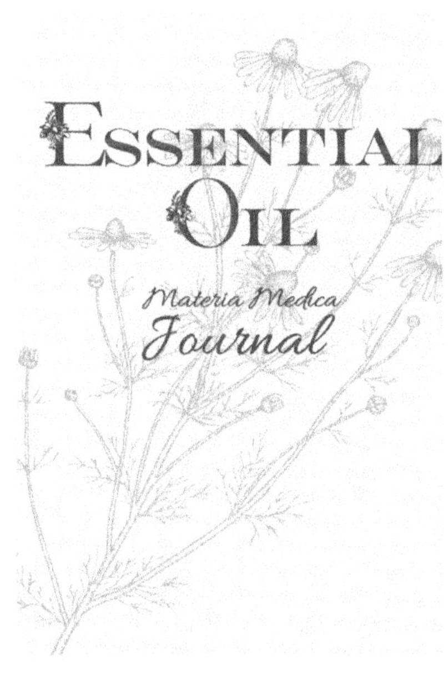

The essential oil materia medica journal continues the tradition of herbalists in documenting the benefits of plants. Creating your own materia medica is a wonderful way to learn more about essential oils.

By journaling the benefits, properties, safety and chemistry of essential oils, you will achieve a deeper understanding of the oils you work with.

This journal has room for 76 profiles and space to enter basic facts, aroma details, properties, chemistry, uses by body system, blending notes, as well as safety and general notes.

Each profile entry is marked with a beautiful botanically decorated letter to help keep things alphabetized, but you can enter any oil profile you want (that is, I don't prescribe which oils you should study). There are 5 blank profiles at the end for any overflow.